3.50

LITTLE SIR HAL KILLIGREW

" The sky may fall and we shall catch larks "

For Hannah and Ben

LĬTTLE·SĬR·HAL KĬLLĬGREW

ELIZABETHAN VOICE IN EUROPE

GILES DARVILL

CRM Publications and Dyllansow Truran

First published in Great Britain 1994
by CRM Publications and Dyllansow Truran
Liberty Walk, Southwell, Nottinghamshire NG25 0EP, UK.

Typesetting by Just-a-Sec, Nottingham

Printed by DESA, Nottingham

ISBN 0 9519706 2 3

CONTENTS

ACKNOWLEDGEMENTS

Little Sir Hal Killigrew draws extensively on the research undertaken by Professor Amos Miller of Houston University, who first revealed Killigrew's remarkable life and thirty years on kindly made valuable suggestions for further study. Professor Paul Hardacre, formerly of Vanderbilt University, also provided useful leads.

Encouragement and practical help were given to the author by Len Truran of Dyllansow Truran.

Assistance in document research was provided by: the British Library and the Public Record Office in London; the Greater London Local History Collection; St. Margaret's Church, Lothbury; Nottingham University Hallward Library; the library at the Royal Institution of Cornwall, Truro; the Local Studies libraries at Redruth, Cornwall, and Hendon, Barnet.

Preface

Little Sir Hal Killigrew

Three of King Henry the Eighth's legitimate children became English Monarchs. Boy King Edward, Bloody Mary and Virgin Queen Elizabeth ruled on God's behalf by Divine Right for over half a century.

Only one Cornish person was close witness of England's Court and Government for the whole of that remarkable period. Henry Killigrew visited Court in the lifetime of Henry VIII and became a young aide of King Edward's most powerful minister. Then he withdrew from officialdom when religious convictions drove him into exile during Queen Mary's Catholic reign: eventually she employed Killigrew in her own service. For forty-five years under Queen Elizabeth he advanced as successful courtier, soldier, spy, foreign diplomat, state interrogator and Exchequer official.

Killigrew always thought of himself as Cornish, buying property in the county, encouraging two of his daughters to marry local gentry, and blaming his Cornish English when the Queen misunderstood his letters. He gave wise counsel when Cornish people needed a word in high places.

During the sixteenth century the Killigrews of Arwennack on the Fal estuary stimulated a mafia of pirates at sea and predators on land. Their coat of arms displayed a two-headed eagle. Henry learnt early to look two ways at once. He never needed to extricate himself from the disreputable side of the family, so totally was he drawn into another world when he married Catherine Cooke, one of five remarkable sisters: other sisters married Elizabeth's chief minister Cecil (Lord Burghley), Lord Chancellor Bacon, and Lord Russell (son of the Earl of Bedford, the West Country's most powerful grandee). These women influenced politics in no small measure and two of their children - Robert Cecil and Francis Bacon - earned lasting fame.

Killigrew's vital diplomatic missions to France, Germany, the Netherlands and Scotland demonstrate how ambassadors and envoys were the fighting edge in Queen Elizabeth's plot to make England great: the military paraded temporarily if diplomacy was forced inshore. Yet his own military knowledge often came in handy.

Killigrew worked closely with most of the greatest figures of the age: Cecil of course, and Elizabeth's favourites Leicester and Essex, also her most formidable hatchet man, the surprisingly admirable Walsingham. He met Mary Queen of Scots in a darkened room and helped to arrange her execution. Francis Bacon was his nephew and he must have known the young Shakespeare.

To execute his missions he sailed the high seas, several times almost drowning, was nearly killed and then captured at a siege of Rouen (where thirty years later he was knighted), rode through forests infested with starving German mercenaries, dug trenches round Edinburgh Castle while under fire, filtered troops past Dutch barricades. He found time to make money and fathered nine children, four of whom were born when he was in his mid to late sixties.

Unlike his own father and most of his brothers, Sir Harry was no unprincipled adventurer, but an active campaigner in a European movement for religious reform. His heart burned for change in worship, ministry and church government, beliefs which sometimes brought him into dangerous conflict with the Queen and probably prevented him from holding office at the very top. However he seems to have been untroubled by ambition.

The story of this remarkable but strangely little known Cornishman was meticulously researched in the 1950s, but Professor Miller's fine and very detailed academic contribution has been out of print for many years. *Little Sir Hal Killigrew*, written for the general reader and historian, summarises that research and adds further findings and reflections of my own.

From Cornwall to London and on to Mantua, Heidelberg and Blois, Killigrew is a very human guide who can be followed into the heart of England's foreign and domestic affairs with their religious and political controversies during fifty crucial years.

KEY DATES

1528 (approx)	Henry Killigrew born
1545	at Greenwich
1547	Henry VIII dies, **Edward VI** succeeds
1549	first trip to Italy
1553	Queen **Mary** succeeds
1555 - 7	mercenary in France
1558	Queen **Elizabeth** succeeds
1561	appointed Teller of the Exchequer
1562 - 3	siege of Rouen, imprisoned in France
1565	marries Catherine Cooke
1569	envoy in German States
1571	resident Ambassador in Paris
1572 - 5	envoy in Scotland
1573	acquires Lanrake
1583	death of Catherine
1585 - 9	in Netherlands with Leicester
1588	Spanish Armada
1590	marries Jaél
1591	in France with Essex, knighted
1592 - 6	fathers four further children
1603	Queen Elizabeth and Killigrew die.

THE CORNISH APPEAL
TO THE QUEEN.

G ranite winds blew the Cornish protest of 1594 along drenched roads to London. Although the Armada had come to grief, war with Spain still edged painfully onwards and would not reach its stale-mate for several years, burdening the county meanwhile with heavy bills and ever-present fear of invasion. Sales of tin were decayed, rain and plague would not abate, and now they must accommodate that 'covetous caterpillar', that 'shifting fellow', the Devil's acolyte Meggs.

Meggs had gone to law to reduce the rights and raise rents of many who occupied Crown land in Cornwall. Having won his law-suit, he was discovering - as he was lynched in the road and his live-stock turned loose - that you could not push your luck with the Cornish on questions of money, especially if you hit rich as well as poor. If God and Queen allowed judgment to stand, security and incomes of ten thousand landowners and cottagers would be affected.

If not God's, certainly Queen Elizabeth's support would have to be worked for. The gentry who decided to appeal directly to the Divinely Appointed Regent were keen to ensure the campaign would not be blown onto rocks like some before it, campaigns which had sunk amid bellowed accusations of treason and rattling of instrumentation for torture and execution. A clear view of the course to be taken, a lightened ship, neatly reefed sails and good leadership would all be needed to prove the petitioners worthy of success. Above all, on this occasion the Cornish would need to make full use of friends at Court, and local leaders should be chosen with this in mind.

Twenty-six years old Jonathan Trelawny was selected to partner Richard Carew at the head of twelve deputies. No stranger to London, he had studied law at the Middle Temple and represented Cornish constituencies in three Parliaments. Although unusually rich for a Cornish gentleman, perhaps his best qualification for this journey was his family connection. This trip to London would be a domestic occasion, and in his baggage no doubt lurked well chosen presents of best Cornish produce. Barrels of conger eels, quince marmalade and a falcon taken from the cliffs?

The Cornishman at Court whose guidance and connections were most essential for this enterprise was Sir Henry Killigrew, former soldier and spy who had spent a life-time as an effective and influential European diplomat and Exchequer official. Although around sixty-five years old in 1594, he was still in a strong position to influence the course of this campaign. Jonathan Trelawny had been brought up as Henry's ward, and then had married Henry's daughter Elizabeth. Among the gifts Jonathan was taking there were likely to be offerings for their grandfather from infant Trelawnys now taking their first steps across lawns at Poole in Menheniot.

The deputation steered its course along the roads to London, finding a harbour in Devon to take on board good advice from Sir Walter Ralegh, formerly Queen Elizabeth's close favourite but now in some disgrace. Ralegh advised them 'not to depend upon the help of many, but principally to solicit the Lord Treasurer, to whom such matters specially appertained'.

If the petitioners had anticipated this advice it might explain why Sir Henry was important to the enterprise. Harry Killigrew moved like an old spider close to the centre of an extensive web which was going to be used. No one else could demonstrate such extensive connections both in Cornwall and among those in Government. He was the principal bridge between two worlds.

The Lord Treasurer was William Cecil, Lord Burghley, who had been maintained by Elizabeth in the most powerful Government positions for nearly forty years - an astonishing unbroken partnership between Sovereign and leading Minister which formed the driving motor of England's advance in war and peace.

Ralegh wrote a letter for the petitioners to hand to Burghley. On the day after their arrival in London Jonathan and others in the deputation visited Sir Henry Killigrew, who, in Carew's words, 'with no less love than great experience gave directions what course was fittest to be followed'. It would be essential to approach both Burghley and the Queen in the appropriate manner. The Court was a dangerous place.

Sir Harry's greatest connection was with Lord Burghley - they were brothers-in-law. Their wives were both now dead and Harry had married again, but this did not diminish the relationship between two men which had lasted over fifty years.

Killigrew and Burghley were now grand survivors, outliving most of their contemporaries. Killigrew's numerous vital missions around Courts and cellars of Europe in the name of God and England had brought advantage to the nation and plentiful rewards to the diplomat. In exchange for Killigrew's loyalty and competence, Burghley had rendered many services.

Twenty two years previously as one reward he had organised for Harry the lucrative wardship of infant Jonathan Trelawny, and later Burghley had taken adolescent Jonathan into his own household - a celebrated civil service college for the highest of young flyers. Jonathan would be looking forward to renewing his acquaintance with this formidable and tetchy giant on the national stage.

Henry too enjoyed direct access to Court, that ever moving forum deemed closer to heavenly judgment than any cathedral. As a Gentleman of the Privy Chamber he was called from time to time to undertake intimate missions for the Queen. His younger brother William also worked at Court, and had held the position of Groom of the Chamber for around twenty years - a less senior post but requiring almost daily attendance upon Her Majesty.

On their second day in London, 6th May, the twelve deputies journeyed down river to Greenwich where the Court was then residing. Greenwich had been Elizabeth's birthplace, and her father's. Predecessor to the one we know, this large palace with three quadrangles built along the river was the setting for the Queen's enjoyment of river sports and water theatricals, hunting and parade of soldiery. The scene too of spectacular falls from Royal favour.

William Killigrew, surely well briefed in advance by his elder brother, stood ready to meet the deputies, and 'advised, argued, served and laboured for them'. He took their letters to the Queen and Burghley, who were particularly impressed by one from Sir Francis Godolphin.

Sir Francis was another key figure in the Killigrew web, so it is perhaps no accident that he turned out a well-judged letter. In Cornwall he was the most influential and richest gentleman of the period. He had chosen not to divide his life between Cornwall and London but rather to concentrate on organising the county against Spain and making money out of tin. His wife, Lady Margaret was sister to Harry and William Killigrew

After two days Jonathan and the others experienced their first meeting with the Lord Treasurer, who still guided political life in the nation and understood the strategic importance of a stable Cornwall during continuing war with Spain.

Several days later their personal audience with the Queen occurred, a carefully prepared and reverential encounter as she emerged in state from the chapel at Greenwich. A German visitor five years later described a similar event: the Queen and her ladies were escorted by the great officers of State and forty swarthy Gentlemen Pensioners - a noble body-guard who were not in those days persons in a retired state. The Queen looked 'very majestic, her face oblong, fair but wrinkled, her eyes small, yet black and pleasant, her nose a little hooked, her lips narrow and her teeth black'. Elizabeth on that day was wearing a pair of fine pearl ear-rings and a small crown topping a red wig. 'Her bosom was uncovered, as all the English ladies have it till they are married: and she had a necklace of exceedingly fine jewels'. She also carried a white silk dress bordered with huge pearls and a black silt mantle threaded with silver. 'Whoever speaks to her, it is kneeling: now and then she raises some with her hand...Wherever she turned her face, as she was going along, everybody fell down on their knees'.

The Cornish, it is recorded, did not fail to kneel with the rest of the crowd delivering their petitions. Elizabeth was expecting to see them, and delivered her verdict on God's behalf concerning the changes in tenancies which had so disrupted the county. 'It shall be remedied. I would they were hanged who have been the doers thereof: for we respect the public more than the private'. The Queen handed responsibility for detailed judgment to the Lord Treasurer.

Perhaps a year or two had passed since Jonathan had last seen the Queen at close quarters. He cannot have failed to notice that her greater frailty had not diminished her formidable political intelligence and acute hold on power. Fear was the currency of survival in this milieu.

The Cornish campaign was not yet won completely, nor would be. Burghley would not concede that the fines (renewal fees payable every seven years) should be fixed in permanence. These were to stay the same for the time being but could be broken in the future - as they would henceforth depend upon the Crown's judgment of what was reasonable. Burghley agreed however, contrary to the previous judgment, that tenants should retain security of tenure. Not a bad outcome. They took their disappointment and concern to Sir Henry Killigrew, who advised them to accept things as they stood 'lest the Lord Treasurer, not easily drawn from his once-taken course, might take some conceit against them'.

Others confirmed this advice and the petitioners set off for Cornwall seven weeks after they arrived. Journeying cannot have been easy: as a contemporary noted, "this year in the month of May fell many showers, but in the months of June and July much more, for it commonly rained every day or night till S. James' Day".

This episode must have added to Jonathan's knowledge of how the Elizabethan state sought to govern. Power was absolute, God and Monarch stood indivisible. Awe dominated the psychology. But if the people accepted these terms - they had little choice - mercy was available, and often made political sense. As historian Rowse summed it up: 'the wish at the top to do justice, to do the best for everybody, manoeuvring for a practical solution to an imprecise, contingent problem which yet could have wide repercussions and make future trouble'.

Writing a few years later about this affair, Carew commented: 'herein we were beholden to Sir Walter Ralegh's ernest writing, to Sir Henry Killigrew's sound advice, and to Master William Killigrew's painful soliciting'.

What would have lodged in Harry Killigrew's mind as he watched the deputation depart from London for the Cornish summer, with Jonathan perhaps laden with presents for the grandchildren? The satisfaction of a professional diplomat who has helped friends to steer away from Satan's rocks of stubborn principle or exaggerated demands?

Henry in his old age enjoyed a second wedding and a young French wife. Having fathered four daughters from his first marriage he was now parenting four more children. Could the encounter have included a more substantial family confrontation? Up to now Henry had resisted any inclination to live in Cornwall; maybe neither of his wives had wished to move, perhaps he had been deterred by the proximity of nephew John, the latest deviant in the Killigrew family, a failed bully still bludgeoning around the Fal River and borrowing money.

In spite of John, would not Cornwall be a good place to rear these new young? Court life and national politics in the mid-nineties were in considerable upheaval. Henry must have felt isolated among a new generation - although characteristically he had made some good connections.

Perhaps the embassy from Jonathan Trelawny, almost an adult son for Henry, was also a family deputation. Did they urge the old man to tack to his point of origin and tie his children to a new Cornish generation? Did he need to give them a further lesson in Tudor politics - that there was no such thing as safe retirement, never any chance of leaving Court without incurring the Queen's hostility and putting all one's gains at risk, never a prospect of moving back to the soft air and clear light of south Cornwall?

THE SCHOOL OF
VIOLENCE AND PRAYER.

Greenwich! Forty-nine years before the visit of the Cornish petitioners, eighteen years old Harry Killigrew journeyed the few winding miles down the River Thames from London to visit that rambling confusion of a Palace: here an elderly Monarch was dwindling out of life.

During 1545 King Henry the Eighth held his Court at Greenwich. Attending was the young man's uncle, Benet Killigrew, Gentleman of the Privy Chamber. Was he looking out when little Hal arrived at the Palace or had such trips become routine?

Young Harry was no doubt performing his professional duties. John Dudley was also in attendance: the country's foremost general, a senior member of the Council and Lord High Admiral. Killigrew was employed among Dudley's gentleman servants: Benet had probably been responsible for finding Hal's place in the Dudley household - already the Killigrew genius for identifying the most useful web and clambering on.

The King was well served by John Dudley, who would need assistance in turn from secretaries and administrators educated in the principles of Tudor power and paranoia, and skilled in riding the tidal wave of divinely sanctioned despotism. Under the King's authority John Dudley's own power, based on his ability and the King's trust, was enhanced because his wife Jane was a lifelong friend of Katherine Parr, the King's latest, sixth and last wife. Catherine and Jane had studied together as children.

Young Killigrew would have approved of the gentle, romantic, persistent Queen Katherine, whose influence at Court enhanced the move towards deeper and broader Protestantism. Her friendships and the appointments she influenced or made reflected her desire for a revived church. John Dudley needed no convincing, like his wife he already shared Katherine's view, and chose secretaries of the same opinions. As a man of action, he was not unusual in having determined views on such matters: in Tudor times there was no habit of splitting sacred and secular.

At Greenwich, Katherine applied herself to softening the tortured development of the two royal children, Prince Edward and Princess Elizabeth. Princess Mary was already a wounded adult. Religious reformers were appointed as tutors to the royal offspring, and the Court had established a small school of ten or so youngsters to surround Edward in his work and play. The Dudleys were not slow to use this opportunity to strengthen their links with the next royal generation, and their twelve years old son Robert was a member of the school; Henry Hasting, future Earl of Huntingdon was another.

Henry Killigrew would not be too proud to glean the latest Court news from his master's son. The Princess Elizabeth was just a few months younger than Robert: she was usually schooled at country houses away from London, but the King's two children sometimes studied together. Katherine Parr had negotiated Elizabeth's rehabilitation at Court: the Princess remained in terrible awe of the King even though he had forgiven her for having former Queen Anne Boleyn as mother. Between Greenwich and Westminster, the grey Tower of London stood to remind Elizabeth that a Monarch's family have to earn their quota of trickled-down divinity.

Elizabeth studied her father's statecraft and stagecraft. While he remained deeply conservative in the essence of his politics and religion, he knew that changes were necessary - as long as these could be introduced under his own control. Why else did he chose a reformer as a wife for his old age, and promote the Dudleys, and allow his Queen to appoint humanist protestants to tutor his long awaited son? Decades later, Elizabeth as Queen would also distrust radical religion but bring in reformers to do much of her business. Perhaps she had already noted the small figure of an ernest Cornishman.

The tone of the King's Court remained constant to his death.

Government would be conducted through fear and implemented through subtle pressure on minds rather than state terror. The Sovereign had taken over the power once held by archbishops and senior barons. God had only one Regent and all who opposed were agents of the Devil. The people were required to remember that the Devil was strong, lurking round every corner with a cup of poison or a dagger, always threatening Crown and State with catastrophe. Any sign of Satan's acolytes must be reported.

If Benet guided his nephew for that visit to Court he might have pointed out the quiet scholarly figure of Sir Anthony Cooke, one of the Prince's tutors. He has chosen to stand aside from the dangerous front-line of paranoid politics and to fight evil more circumspectly.

Like other tutors Cooke was deeply imbued with the new humanistic religion and the wider cultural renaissance which was identified with Cambridge. The young people in his charge absorbed the New Learning, including the messages in Bishop Latimer's fiery Protestant sermons condemning the luxury and corruption of the Court. The astute might have noted that doctrinal opinions were not undergoing much change: for example Cooke and many others still believed in the transubstantiation of the bread into flesh during the Mass.

The young people at Court received a broad education, which included hearing from John Leland about his visitations to the counties of England. Perhaps his account included the story of his trip to Cornwall in 1538 when he visited the Killigrew's house at Arwennack, no doubt receiving from Sir John Killigrew a view of the proposed site of Pendennis Castle, and perhaps meeting an alert ten year old preparing for his travels.

Benet Killigrew and Sir Anthony Cooke surely knew one another: as well as a tutor to the King, Cooke was one of the 'spears', the Royal Bodyguard. He was already renowned for his five formidable daughters, one of whom in that year married William Cecil, a rising Court official.

Princess Elizabeth did not come to the throne of England for another thirteen years, but already as a twelve year old she moved around in a circle which contained key names who would predominate in her own long reign - Cecil, Dudley, Hastings, also

Nicholas Throckmorton - standard bearers of reform who risked their lives in loyalty to Tudors.

Elizabeth's circle glowed like a halo: Henry Killigrew must have resolved to stay in its comfort with no illusions about its capacity to burn as well as to warm. Harry's own professional and private circle of later years was also centred on many of the same names, Cecil, Throckmorton and Hastings were older than him, the Princess and Dudley younger. Was he already aware of Catherine Cooke, another special child lit by the radiance from these figures, the youngest of Sir Anthony's clever daughters, although she probably did not come to Court in those years?

Henry not only absorbed personal contacts. His own deep religious radicalism was founded in the formidable school of Latimer, royal tutors such as Cooke, Cheke and Ascham (lover of books and blood-sports). A very English radicalism: intellectual rather than emotional in content, allied to property interests, spreading from the top downwards - this national style contrasted with Calvin's Swiss reformation with its roots in the day to day practice of popular religion. However, it shared a sense of the frantic struggle between Good and Evil, the fateful dependence of the individual on God's will, the loneliness of the sinful soul waiting guiltily for God's forgiveness.

The Dudleys unlocked the door to the world of power for Killigrew. From the windows at Greenwich they could look back past the cold Tower of doom to their own Ely Palace, between Westminster and the City of London, another rambling building with magnificent gardens. Here Henry must have lived since he was a boy, accompanying the older Dudley children in their learning. Lessons were not all sermons warning of the Devil's assaults on country and conscience. A pupil was taught many ways to fight for God: to ride, handle a rapier, be smart with buckler and dagger, shoot with bow and arrow, fly a hawk and don a suit of armour to wield sword, pike and staff.

Henry may also have studied at Cambridge, but if so no record of this has been traced, although he later endowed Emmanuel, a reforming college. His fluency in Italian and French and his knowledge of classical literature could have been acquired elsewhere.

In the year before the trip to Greenwich, aged sixteen or thereabouts, he had probably already enjoyed his first experience of military action. In 1544 he may have followed his master the Lord High Admiral in the divinely sanctioned devastation of Edinburgh, and witnessed English atrocities there. He may too have joined the 40,000 men who laid siege to Bologne in France: here John Dudley lost a son, and the leading Cornishman William Godolphin excelled himself. Nicholas Throckmorton was in Edinburgh and Bologne.

On either mission Henry might have been torn between a desire to fight and a duty to contribute to the formidable administration of the campaigns, which was an area where Dudley was not fully competent and therefore relied heavily on those around him. The Devil could otherwise always get into the details.

Henry may also have undertaken administrative duties in support of Dudley's role as Lord High Admiral, which involved hearing complaints about piracy, evasion of harbour dues and plundering of wrecks. As a Killigrew Henry would understand these matters: poacher's son now gamekeeper for the state.

In 1547 after King Henry died painfully, the ten year old became King Edward the Sixth. Still tutored by Cooke, he relied heavily on two or three of his senior ministers, including John Dudley. Robert Dudley remained a key companion to the King and still saw Princess Elizabeth.

For some years things went well for John Dudley and his circle, before the power struggles around King Edward became more vicious than usual. Dudley was relaxed enough to allow his gentleman servant the luxury of a trip abroad.

In 1549, when he was around twenty-one, Henry Killigrew visited Italy. Education and diplomacy as well as enjoyment may have been goals of the trip. Italy was both admired for its culture and feared for its political and religious inclinations. A young Englishman needed to understand at first hand what might be brewing in the peninsula of Popes. Meanwhile he would improve his Italian, every European's second tongue and the language of diplomacy.

In January, slightly younger Thomas Hoby was entertaining himself in Padua and in his journal he recalls how he and Henry travelled together to Mantua and the Po valley. They witnessed the arrival in Mantua of Prince Philip, accompanied by a thousand horse: later, as King of Spain, Philip tussled with English queens for fifty years and came to embody an Englishman's Antichrist.

Hoby's activities give clues to how Henry too must have passed the time of day and night. Hoby learnt Italian - which he later put to brilliant use in his famous translation of Castiglione's *The Courtier* - and also Latin, was lectured in civil law and logic. He enjoyed the statuary and architecture, and pleasure gardens whose orange trees could be moved in their tubs. He followed deadly Italian feuds and scandalous murders, and stayed on into 1550, travelling to Sicily.

The young men surely talked of all these matters and did not fail to compare Italian women with English. It became clear later that they shared the same taste for the clever rather austere type now emerging in England, and perhaps even then staked hopeful claims on their preferred Cooke sisters.

Political events in England probably triggered Henry's return. Civil strife fully engaged the Dudleys during 1549. Rebellions against inconsistent weak rule of another minister - the King's evil counsellor - broke out in several parts of England. Robert Dudley, now sixteen and no doubt eager for action, was commissioned to join his father in suppressing the insurgents, and took youthful and not very effective action in East Anglia. Henry too was probably involved in some way in this conflict between Englishmen, whose grievances on either side could have been solved in a tidier age without the carnage which ensued. In Tudor England conflict was Absolute, every skirmish became drawn into the cosmic struggle between Heaven and Hell.

There was a notable outbreak of rebellion in Cornwall, focussed on the reformed Prayer Book. Cornishmen took sides, as ever. The Devil might literally have taken your neighbour - into his service. Henry's uncle on his mother's side, William Trewynnard, who earlier in the year had to pawn plate and jewellery to meet creditors, had his lands ravaged and his goods despoiled by rebels. Forced to take refuge at St. Michael's Mount, he was attacked and - according to one account - he lost his life.

As one outcome of these troubles John Dudley became the foremost person in England, but he had not sought this responsibility. He is one of the unfairly maligned figures of the sixteenth century, a committed statesman whose moderate ambition was not propelled by an inflated view of his abilities. He wanted to safeguard the realm - its borders, wealth and religion - from the European and largely Catholic enemies who always sought to fill a vacuum with their evil ways. His mistake was to fail: a Monarch can do no wrong, counsellors must take the rap.

By the time Henry Killigrew was twenty one or twenty two he found himself in the service of the most powerful person in the land; even Princess Elizabeth was beholden to Dudley for the quality of her life.

Now Duke of Northumberland, Killigrew's master watched over King Edward well during these years, and Harry's political and wider education continued as he made more acquaintances at Court and elsewhere. Often the Council met at Dudley's palace. The Duke maintained his solicitude for Princess Elizabeth, giving over his house at Hatfield for her use. Cecil, who had successfully walked the tightrope between rival factions, was dispatched as her surveyor. William and Mildred Cecil had recently presented the Cookes with their first grandchild.

Henry was probably already involved in European diplomacy. One of his acquaintances, or perhaps a friend, was François de Vendome, a French nobleman who was Vidame of Chartres. He was one of three who in 1550 were part of an education exchange scheme whereby youthful English and French aristocrats swopped places in their respective Courts. The Vidame was a member of King Edward's schoolroom and seems to have lived with the Dudleys. He was a boon companion of the King, often urging him to abandon his books for more favoured sporting pastimes. François too will reappear in the Killigrew story.

Still in his early twenties Killigrew must have begun to recognise the importance, as a younger son, of becoming financially established. He acquired newly released monastic lands at Blackfriars in Truro, and was awarded the post of havenor or harbour-master of the Duchy of Cornwall. This was no doubt an office which could be made lucrative, and may have involved him in the scrutiny of his Cornish family's more unscrupulous enterprises. He also became bailiff of the manor of Helston, and in 1553 sat as Member of Parliament for Newport juxta Launceston, as one of a raft of nominees whereby Dudley sought to pack the benches with supporters on the politically correct side of the cosmic divide.

It was obvious that the unfortunate King was dying, and Dudley became involved in the plot of 1553 - muddled and half-hearted rather than Machiavellian - to prevent the unmarried Princesses, either Catholic Mary or Protestant Elizabeth, from assuming the crown. The consequences of marriage between a female Monarch and a foreigner were widely feared. Dudley persuaded the dying young King and the Council to agree to the marriage of one of his own very English sons to the minor royal Lady Jane Grey, an act which led on Edward's death to her proclamation as Queen.

The Dudleys, including Robert, attempted military action in support of this venture. Henry may have doubted the wisdom of all this, and Cecil seems to have played a double game, not for the last time. However, the very fact that the Council were prepared to agree to the plan indicates the depth of English fear of foreigners, the sense of surrounding danger and imminent catastrophe which was the normal backdrop of politics.

Princess Mary won this contest. For John Dudley things came to a sticky head under the axe, and Robert was under sentence of death for a while. Sir Anthony Cooke took his books and his dignity into the Tower, accused of a role in the plot. Henry seems to have convinced everyone that his nose was clean, and rather than run for cover he remained in the Dudley household after the Duke's execution. Perhaps he hoped that the new Queen Mary would adopt sensible Tudor policies and safeguard recent reforms. Maybe he was encouraged to stay in situ to ensure reliable intelligence for Cecil and others while they crossed safely from one regime to another.

Direct evidence of Killigrew's idealism has survived only from later in his life, but King Edward's unhappy reign had provided many lessons on the twists and turns of understanding which are required when God and Monarch are indivisible. Princess Elizabeth had also observed these developments, noting the kind Northumberland's willingness to name her a bastard and exclude her from the throne, and the keenness of other devotees to risk her life in their cause.

The next fifty years demonstrated that Killigrew and Elizabeth drew rather different conclusions from these events. They both shared Dudley's pre-occupation with strong internal government and national security, but Elizabeth developed a keener eye for the danger of political or military initiatives. God might seem to be demanding action, but perhaps this was the Devil's trick. When zeal and storms, disease and insolvency were so unpredictable and could lead you so far astray, let others take action first. From religious reform too she sensed perils as well as benefits, especially when any change risked a challenge to the convenient association between Heaven and the Court.

Elizabeth had five further years to wait before her formidable era of power: five years while her elder sister repeated all the recent mistakes and added her own with dogma and incense.

Was the twenty-five year old Cornishman already smouldering with religious fire? If so, would he conceal his passion or ignite in consuming flames?

LONELY IN
THE INFERNO

T he years of Queen Mary's dark rule must have appeared to Henry like a hangover induced by the excesses of a long celebration. Fond company vanishes as the dawn transforms every person you encounter into a grotesque beast of myth wriggling to get out of its niche.

King Edward and Princess Elizabeth, humanist royal tutors, Dudleys and other reformers, the raft of Cooke sisters, ebullient Nicholas Throckmorton, the Court and its richly varied human spectacle lived out beside the Thames - all have disappeared. Monarchy itself seems to have submitted to the Evil Eye. The world of retreat and rebellion also seems peopled with the unbalanced or reluctant, friends who openly change sides or become treasonable double-agents, like pirates sailing from a dark estuary to espouse any cause.

During the years leading up to Henry's thirtieth birthday, his bestiary gave sickening birth to many valuable and life-enduring lessons - as many as the gilded court had bred. Yet while Killigrew encountered these hellish creatures he may have found little pattern or meaning by reflecting on their gestures.

At the start of the reign he must have hoped that essentials would stay the same. Then he tried to believe that a successful rebellion against Mary's Evil Counsellors would force her to change her ways or would lead to her replacement by Princess Elizabeth. When this scenario failed to materialise he was concerned with little more than survival in a hostile foreign environment, hoping only for an act of God which would remove a Tudor Queen whom he probably now despised.

Did he even have doubts, did he wonder if the cause he fought for was the just one? To be sure, Henry's problem was to locate the Enemy. Mary's marriage to Philip of Spain effectively subjugated England as a colony and led to several hopeless rebellions, including another in the West Country. Most reformers held that Spain and Catholicism could not be allowed to seep into the land. Those Protestants, either driven by ideals to seek allies overseas or hounded out and forced to run for their own safety, increased in numbers to a considerable trickle but never to a stream.

Into that flow went Killigrew, also tutors Cheke and Cooke. Throckmorton had a worrying spell in the Tower and then followed them abroad. Others were less sure where the Devil lurked: Cecil almost began to look like a Catholic and Robert Dudley hedged uneasily.

Before Henry went into exile he may have set off for a brief visit to Cornwall, leaving behind the River Thames and the spooky Tower of London. Ahead of him the wide estuary of the Fal.

Yndan An Fala - valley beneath the sea. England's largest natural harbour was wardened by his family's house and the two new castles of Pendennis and Mawes. His early childhood!

Memories! The outer landscape which he held in his mind was centred on the fortified house of Arwennack. Harry's first play area must have been the courtyard surrounded by walls as high as the sky. The original house seems to have been integrated with the square of defensive walls surmounted at each corner by a higher circular turretted tower. You looked through the courtyard gate onto the wide estuary garnished with scrub oak.

Below the house on rocky beaches turnstones searched among debris of prawns victimised by baby cuttlefish and pretty anemones. Children gathered the littering bones of adult cuttlefish who had wired their eggs to the eel-grass and died.

As Carew wrote two generations later, "Arwennack entertaineth you with a pleasing view, for the same standeth so far within the haven's mouth that it is protected from the sea storms, and yet so near unto as it yieldeth a ready passage out; besides the cliff on which the house abutteth is steep enough to shoulder off the waves and the ground about it plain and large enough for recreation".

Pendennis a mile away on the headland looked out to sea and across the wide mouth of the estuary towards Mawes: these were outposts of King Henry the Eighth's line of new coastal defences. Built when Henry Killigrew was a boy Pendennis was commissioned in 1543 with his father as the first Governor.

Below the cliffs greedy bleny, ugly goby, touchy wrasse (that Cornish name) and weaver fish poisonous to handle made their carefree livings on the tissue of weaker neighbours.

Henry was born around 1528. What was the inner landscape of his childhood? He was the fourth of five sons and had five sisters. His father Sir John and three elder brothers were all tough men of action, predators, the eyes of both eagles' heads fixing their glare upon the weak, always ready for bending or breaking the law when it pleased them and quick in attack when threatened by neighbours' interests.

The inner landscape was always at the mercy of events. The Killigrews could never forget that perils might suddenly assail them. The estuary had been a befouled nest of pirates for decades, many of them friends of father Sir John. The conflicts of the wider world imploded from time to time: Henry is unlikely to have left for London before the winter of 1537 when a Spanish fleet chased four French vessels past astonished Arwennack and trapped them at Truro near the head of the twisting estuary.

When you were still as young as eight or nine, a boy of promise from the gentry could be sent to be page in the household of an aristocrat or rising official. Here you would be educated and if promise was fulfilled you became a gentlemen servant. Other Cornish boys followed this path, George and other children of Honor Basset for example. In their new homes their personalities might be fostered or assaulted: from the story of the Basset children revealed in their parents' papers - the Lisle Letters - it is clear that some parents chose homes with as much care as grandees chose their pages.

Disjunctures between roughness in the Killigrew household and sophistication at John and Jane Dudley's at Ely Palace in the 1540s can only have disrupted the sense of the world which young Henry, as a nine or ten year old, was piecing together. However, these disjunctures should not be exaggerated: both households must have shared the fundamental paranoia of the age, the sense of dependence on the absolute Monarch, the fear of foreigners and neighbours who might be serving the Devil's latest cause and threatening to undermine you with false testimony.

Each family had to shift for itself. The Arwennack style was not exceptional but shared its behaviour with all classes. As the historian Stone wrote, this behaviour was characterised by 'ferocity, childishness and lack of self control... to quarrel was a moral duty'. The Dudleys had more surface refinement, but could shift for themselves at the highest level: it was not sweetness which brought them so close to absolute power.

To keep himself together when he left his mother and family Henry packed all his Cornish kin into his young soul as if they were souvenirs and carried them away to his new home between the City of London and Westminster. He crammed into his variegated personality every character in the Killigrew cast, to draw out when needed in the dangerous yards of Court. His roots in south-west Cornwall nourished the astonishing combination of aptitudes which finally emerged: in spying and finance, religious zealotry and state murder, scholarship, soldiery and supervision in the torture chamber, family leadership and wandering, puritanism and sexual marathon running.

These Killigrew roots ran deep, but like many of the old Celtic gentry with Cornish pedigrees which crossed many generations, their wealth was less impressive. The family only emerged from obscurity by whole-heartedly adopting Protestantism during the first religious reforms and profiting from the dissolution of monasteries and chantries. Probably they had no choice - if you did not grab what was on offer (in the name of God) your neighbour would do so.

The contrast between legality and illegality was as blurred as it can be today in an area dominated by a mafia of organised terror. Henry's father displayed many of the characteristics of a Godfather, accepting official responsibilities for civil government, including control of piracy, whilst continuing to bend or disregard the law. In this he did not differ from grandees fighting for the heart and mind of King Edward or squaring up to European politics.

Tudor monarchs had little choice but to tolerate such local practices. For much of the sixteenth century Cornwall was an exposed front line against hostile powers. France and Spain, always a threat to England, did not scruple to use Ireland in addition to the Channel as fronts for aggression or subversion. Cornwall's long coastline was almost impossible to defend, and much Cornish wealth was spent in the attempt.

The Crown could only with difficulty be persuaded to take seriously the defence of the county, preferring instead to milk it of revenue through the Duchy. They disregarded the deviant behaviour of any local leader able to demonstrate commitment to coastal defence and civil order in times of special peril.

A blind eye turned to stolen goods deriving from piracy and privateering - booty which at times must have crammed Pendennis - was a price the Crown seemed willing to pay. There were few Cornish gentleman and their ladies who was not deeply into the same business, or else too frightened to act against it.

The Killigrews attempted to establish legitimate trade too, by building up the Fal as a complement to Fowey and Plymouth further east. It is a mistake to see the Killigrews as rough pirates with a veneer of respectability. Uncle Benet had already achieved eminence at the Tudor Court. Henry's mother was a Trewynnard whose recent ancestors included at least one senior church dignitary. Henry's sister Margaret married the heir of one of the richest and most respected families in the county, the Godolphins (themselves not above encouraging a little piracy). Young Francis Godolphin, like Henry, was a deeply educated and sensitive man. The Godolphin family had no need to ally themselves with the Killigrews unless the latter had earned the right to be taken seriously.

Cornish gentry displayed a strong sense of family and all his life Henry remained in contact with his relations, returning home at intervals and seeing them in London. Given his later fondness for military action it is easy to picture him on a youthful visit to his parents in summer - taking part in devious maritime forays under the guidance of his elder brothers and gathering intelligence from taverns and churchyards to assist his father's assertions against rivals.

If Henry journeyed to Cornwall around 1554, as the glum rabbitty

Mary was strengthening the Catholic counter-reformation in England, he would have found much discontent which might soon bubble up. Perhaps he was still deciding whether or not to pay the price of revolt and possible exile.

We can do no more than guess Henry's motives for going into France. Was he an idealist seeking allies, or was he a fugitive for his life, or perhaps the two together? He may have delayed his decision about exile to see the outcome of the first wave of rebellions, but found himself implicated in these beyond redemption, leaving himself with no choice but to go abroad. West Country rebellion was badly led and inadequately supported. Henry is quite likely to have been involved when his brothers provided an escape route to France for one of its leaders, but the whole campaign was scarcely worthy of credible support.

Meanwhile Robert Dudley remained in the Tower, and was finally released in great financial difficulties, while his brother was executed. Princess Elizabeth was also taken to the Tower - that place where her mother had been so unjustly beheaded. Queen Mary's marriage to the King of Spain went ahead, the Catholic party was ascendant. To radical Protestants the Devil had won.

Rebellions of that reign failed because people of influence did not trust drastic methods of political change. Like Elizabeth they had learnt the dangers of action and hoped that less forcible means could curb Mary, and foresaw only chaos from her overthrow, even if she was replaced by Princess Elizabeth. Gentry and business classes, although mostly Protestants, wanted demilitarisation, trade and order. To some extent alliance with Catholic Spain promised these against the greater peril of Catholic France. Most rebels too were motivated more by financial grievances or blistering anti-clericalism - complaints where small changes might make a big difference - than by a desire to sail on a pilgrimage of Protestantism.

If Harry was already a zealot he was required to trawl his ideals through a pond of churned brown banality. When he fled to France the quality of his companions deteriorated without remission. The French sought to use presence on their soil of English rebels in order to advance their own national and Catholic interests against England. Henry's brothers, led by Peter, were lent Sacrette and other ships by the French King in order to harrass the Spanish up and down the Channel. As usual muddling politics and cupidity, they sought to profiteer from the state of affairs. Henry advised them to steer clear of the French and return home, presumably preferring more subtle diplomacy and subterfuge to bring down the English government.

Peter landed in the Tower when his ships were captured after a battle with the English navy. Henry was not on board, but Sir John was implicated and deprived of his Governorship. Under duress no doubt, Peter gave the Government useful information, and was encouraged to change sides and sail for the Queen, after which Sir John was restored.

Henry continued to distance himself from his family. He was sent by the rebel leaders on a journey to Italy, first visited seven years earlier, where he sounded out the Earl of Devon as a possible figurehead for revolt, but this young man turned into a toad and promptly drowned in his own mediocrity.

Henry was now a penniless refugee. However doubtful he may have felt initially about exile, his actions from this point confirm the soundness of his commitment to radical reform, in spite of the cost. Many exiles were now finding ways to make peace with Mary, and the Exchequer and spy-masters were glad to help them ease their passage home. His own offences were not too great for forgiveness, provided his penitence was accompanied by useful information. Yet he remained in France, considerably disadvantaged.

Killigrew encountered a griffin from his own gilded past, the Vidame of Chartres, and for three years entered his service, fighting among French Protestants against that greater enemy the Spanish. At home Robert Dudley made uncomfortable peace with the Queen and King Philip, and set about recruiting a force to fight for Spain: this army included Throckmorton. Mercenaries on opposite sides, fighting at St Quentin in 1557 for foreign powers whose interest in England was uncertain! At this battle Henry offered brief assistance to James Melville, whom he encountered many times in Scotland in years ahead.

How Princess Elizabeth must have become the focus of all their hopes! Released from the Tower she avoided the suicide of open involvement in any plots against the Queen. Jackdaw King Philip was more interested in long term friendship with England than his wife's happiness, and hedged his bets by acting with solicitude towards the Princess. Cecil continued to survey on her behalf, his nose poked up like a seal in a bay, and he swam in and out of Mary's gaze as well. No dangerous fights on French soil for him.

Queen Mary's slaughter of English Protestants took fire during the final years of her reign. If Henry's loathing of her regime deepened so did his helplessness.

After the Spanish victory at St Quentin, Killigrew had nothing to gain by further antagonising the English government, and stayed away from English conspirators and French opportunists. It was not capitulation, he could probably have bought his way home, but did not do so. He moved to Strasbourg, where Sir Anthony Cooke was perched in much more comfortable exile, like a damp owl in a warm loft, writing pamphlets and supplying information to Cecil - for which no doubt he was paid.

Young Hoby, Henry's friend from Italy, was firmly in England, and had married the formidable Elizabeth Cooke in June 1558. Margaret Cooke had also married, to a rich courtier and merchant, but died within a few weeks of the wedding.

Eventually Henry was given a mysterious commission, apparently on the initiative of Queen Mary but with the knowledge of Princess Elizabeth. He was asked to go into France, probably to use his military judgment and good relations with the Protestant faction, of which the Vidame of Chartres was a leading member, in order to discover the strength of the Popish French and their intentions against England.

Elizabeth's involvement in planning this mission is strange, as she was only on the margins of power. Perhaps the Queen had called on her sister's influence with Protestants in England and France.

Before this venture could bear any fruit, Queen Mary was dead.

From the impenetrable quagmire of her reign Henry rose like a hungry fish-eagle with hope in his talons. These years had displayed on a wider canvas what he saw in miniature at Arwennack and later at Ely House under the shadow of King Henry and the Dudleys: the realities of politics. The sixteenth century was the first age of government by paper, but the top diplomat needed those other skills too; professional soldiery, the art of spying, a clear view of the perfidy of overseas rivals and the treachery of conspirators.

In half a decade of schooling these lessons required Hal to endure, listen and accept. Five years in the prime of his adulthood without home, landscape, family or even any money.

Yet out of his experience the strongest distillation was Harry's vision - a glare, not a glimmer. From the corpse of dead forms of religion would spring not a torrent of worldliness nor the death of God and stench of spiritual emptiness for man; rather a purged and resurrected religion, glowing in the warmth of its simple accessibility for the honest worshipper.

Long live Elizabeth! If Henry had learnt some of the diplomat's operational skills, had he also absorbed more strategic lessons? Had not Mary's reign confirmed the lessons from Edward's: the need for great caution at home and abroad, the importance of political consensus and a fusion of ideas? These lessons required the diplomat to hesitate before dividing the world into simple categories of Good and Evil: required in short a political consciousness which outstripped the languages available to Catholic or Calvinist.

Here Elizabeth and her exiled followers parted company. It is hard to be moderate when you have paid for your ideals with five years of your life. Many turns of Mary's reign had confirmed that John Dudley was correct to fear the power of English Catholicism. But were the apparent extremes of Genevan protestantism any less dangerous to the stability of the realm and the safety of the crown? Had not these Marian rebels endangered Elizabeth's own life by seeking to implicate her in their conspiracies? Could she ever trust them again?

A Tudor monarch was glad of the people's wide acceptance of her Divine Right to power, and their readiness to fight when she identified the threatening Devil within or without. However, she could not always be expected to mow down every domestic or overseas demon which a religious zealot might find lurking under a stone or on a hilltop.

As she assumed power the Queen realised that extremists still wished to push her into confrontation. Cooke broke out piously: "If the Queen, mindful of the great mercy she has received, will but place her confidence in God; if she will daily say unto the Lord, 'Thou are my fortress, my rock, and my refuge', there will neither be wanting to herself the spirit of a Judith or a Deborah, nor wisdom to her counsellors, nor strength to her army". He soon revealed the plans God had for her.

A romantic rebel like Henry sustained himself on religious ideals, at all times wanting those in power to hear what God was saying to them. His Swiss God had little understanding of consensus, fusion of opposites, caution in action. Killigrew's vision was deeply admirable and widely dangerous.

When Henry came back across the Channel in the autumn of 1558 his first thought must have been not Judith's spirit but the rebuilding of his shattered career. Could he hope for a reward for his sacrifices? He had proved his loyalty to the new Queen; would her miraculous spirit reward this loyalty?

In an ambitious moment he may have ranked himself equal in experience to one such as Cecil who, for all his advantage of age and office, had never worked or even travelled abroad or served in an army. Unlike Robert Dudley, greatly his superior in status, he had remained unambiguously true to his Protestantism. Could he not gaze with self-respect and pride into anyone's eyes, and hope for a fine future as a servant of his ideals?

THE OFFICIAL AGENT.

The new reign's enemies spelt out danger at home and abroad, but the weaponry required against them was subtlety. Throckmorton, Cooke, Killigrew and many others were hoping to occupy useful offices in London, buttressed in their endeavours perhaps by gifts of land confiscated from Mary's supporters.

Henry was soon to be given important diplomatic work, but substantial recognition eluded him for two years. The Queen and Cecil felt that many of these returning exiles were too personally identified with reform to provide the balanced judgment required during this transitional period. None of the most energetic or idealistic among the Marian exiles ever obtained high office.

Cecil! Elizabeth relied for advice on one man above all others as she established her rule: her Principal Secretary. They reinforced each other in caution. Cecil always put first the good of Sovereign and realm, but a second consideration was the maintenance of his own power. The appointment of Throckmorton as Ambassador in Paris - an important but not pre-eminent post - probably showed Cecil's desire to get a rival away from Court, certainly Throckmorton thought so. Cecil claimed to be concerned about Nicholas' alleged unreliability and extreme opinions.

Some anticipated that Cooke might be appointed to the important post of Lord Chancellor, but the Cornish born Bishop Jewel of Salisbury - who had also been in exile - thought him ill-equipped for the post. The job went to one of his sons in law, Ann's husband Nicholas Bacon. In the first Elizabethan parliament Cooke began to take a very strong line on religious reform, which put him in disfavour with the Queen.

While in London Henry must have passed on many occasions the spot where Bishops Ridley and Latimer had been burnt to death by Mary for their Protestant views. Latimer in particular was a great social and religious thinker whose influence on Henry's generation of radicals was decisive. No doubt too Harry reinforced himself with news from Cornwall of the continued need for reforms of the Church in the county. Bishop Jewel wrote of his own diocese nearby: "It is hardly credible what a harvest, or rather what a wilderness of superstition had sprung up in the darkness of Marian times. We found in all places votive relics of saints, nails with which the infatuated people dreamed that Christ had been pierced, and I know not what small fragments of the sacred cross. The number of witches and sorceresses had everywhere become enormous. If inveterate obstinacy was found anywhere, it was altogether among the priests". Jewel himself in years to come was not above acquiring substantial wealth but would have deplored how in 1561 a fifth of Cornwall's people were foisted with absentee clergy, many holding numerous livings.

Foreign affairs presented even greater challenges. As soon as Elizabeth was settled on the throne she began the urgent process of sorting out her relationship with countries of mainland Europe. To aid her in this process she needed diplomats who were trustworthy, competent and willing to travel.

England's political aims in the second half of the sixteenth century are not complicated. Although there are continuous shifts of detail which give the appearance of complexity, the main outline remains consistent for over forty years.

The over-riding aim was to achieve England's security from attack and colonisation. The secondary aim was to create opportunities for expansion, especially for trade and the country's own overseas colonisation.

To achieve security England had to consider the two most powerful powers, France and Spain, either of whom might be actively hostile. However, each of these two would be likely to prevent the other from dominating England. To forestall attack England had therefore to look for opportunities - for example through an alliance with one or the other - to preserve that balance. At times England had to avoid the further danger that the two might co-operate in hostility.

England's immediate consideration was to prevent France from extending a powerful foothold in Scotland. Later in the reign the predominant aim was to prevent either France or Spain becoming too powerful in the Netherlands (approximately today's Holland and most of Belgium).

During Elizabeth's long reign the balance of power shifted as Spain outstripped France. Spain controlled important parts of Europe, including the Netherlands, and was the key power in the Caribbean and northern parts of South America - which provided the wealth to pursue an aggressive foreign policy.

A key dimension during the whole period was religion. Spain was almost completely Catholic, and sought to undermine Protestantism as long as actions to that end did not hinder its own interests. In countries other than Spain internal religious conflict existed. France, which might otherwise have rivalled Spain, was increasingly split by religion - although Catholics were usually dominant: this division hindered its capacity to stand up to Spain and expand into the New World and beyond. Internal religious conflicts - in France, Scotland, the Netherlands and to a lesser extent in England - meant that religious factions within each country would sometimes look abroad for support against their own rulers.

Aspects of Elizabeth's genius included the depth of her understanding of the European situation, and her realism. She recognised from the outset that her opportunities for expansion were limited and possible outcomes of aggressive foreign policy were usually too dangerous to risk. She also prevented religion from over-taking political and economic interests, concentrating instead on security, diplomacy and use of minimum force.

In 1558 England was encircled. Its population was quite small, even by 1600 only four and a half million compared to nine million in Spain/Portugal and sixteen million in France. A real danger at this time was that the French and Spanish would ally and split power between them - including sharing the flesh and bones of England, possibly in powder form. France had close links and considerable influence with Scotland, in spite of growing Protestantism there. The Netherlands, which contained Antwerp, England's main trading artery with the rest of the world, were in Spanish hands. The German states were partly under Spanish influence.

So the main task for Elizabeth was to explore ways of playing Spain and France like two sails working against each other to hold the hove-to position, whilst she appeared if possible to comply with these two powers: she tried also to form mutually advantageous alliances with sympathetic elements in as many countries as possible. The Netherlands, Scotland and Germany were beginning to produce anti-colonial rebellions, with a strong but not exclusively anti-Catholic flavour. French Protestants - Huguenots - were a growing force.

Stealth was needed, based on good intelligence. One of the most urgent tasks was to get in touch with some of the key Protestant leaders whose domains bordered on the French and Spanish spheres of influence. These included the German States. Contact had to be made with the Elector of the Palatinate, based in Heidelberg, and with the Duke of Wurttemberg in Stuttgart.

The English needed a diplomat who could work in secret, for fear of disrupting simultaneous peace approaches to France and Spain. Was there a man who already possessed experience and credibility in Germany, based on firm Protestant convictions, and a proven record of caution and discretion? Henry Killigrew's first official mission came as Elizabeth's first envoy.

Henry's toes, shins and knees waded in the current of European affairs - always taking care not to step on the spines of the weaverfish. As the news of his appointment spread to his family in Cornwall, he must have felt currents of responsibility, ambition and excitement swirling round his thighs. This work suited his zeal. As the historian Smith put it "despite Machiavelli, diplomacy was still perceived far less as the delicate balancing of political goals and economic means than as a dynastic clash of right versus wrong".

His first official mission established useful links, providing the government with helpful information about German politics and scope for hiring mercenaries, but did not go much further. Henry was clearly testing how far English policy could be pushed towards firm offensive alliances with Protestant powers, and he sometimes exceeded his brief. The new Queen and Cecil learnt to become wary of the more militant Protestants among those ministers and ambassadors who saw things too plainly in terms of God and the Devil. Discreetly supported by Robert Dudley (an increasingly influential courtier and favourite of the Queen) the radicals began to form a lobby.

In 1559 Henry was one of several envoys dispatched for negotiations with France over the recovery of the Channel port of Calais and wider matters. These were complementary to official tripartite talks involving Spain as well, so as in Germany they must be treated as sub rosa. Even so, might France play a double game and betray the English to the Spanish?

This diplomacy achieved little for England, and the young Elizabeth began to show her capacity for violent condemnation of diplomats who failed her. Killigrew was not this time in the firing line, but the warning had been given: she was her father's daughter.

Life for an active diplomat, or any politician, had fewer pleasures than may be imagined. As Smith continued: "it is difficult to catch the emotional flavour of Tudor politics, the inner and hidden spasms that gripped the bowels, the sleepless nights of worry, and above all the unpredictable oscillation between frantic haste and endless waiting demanded of those who served the mulish whims and inconstant humours of the powerful".

Killigrew, along with many English Protestants including Cooke and some members of the Council, had become convinced by now that a secret pact existed between France and Spain for the extermination of Protestantism. This theory - which was substantially correct - continued to provide him with an understanding of the conflicts which later occurred. It fuelled his eagerness to subvert Catholic governments and made him ready to exaggerate the hostility of Catholic rulers. In Elizabeth's analysis however, economic and dynastic differences between France and Spain would always override any convergence over religion, and mostly that was so.

Harry was given no time to settle his private life. Later in 1559 the energetic bachelor was returned to France as secretary to his friend Throckmorton, England's first resident Ambassador, whose ability and experience had now decisively recommended themselves to Elizabeth and Cecil - in disregard of his opinions.

Nicholas had requested Harry's presence for the Byzantine negotiations with the French: he became the first to recognise and actively promote Killigrew's career. Soon Dudley would value Killigrew's support within the actively Protestant faction, and it was not long thereafter that Cecil too, faced with more national work to be undertaken than talent to recruit, sought to advance him and underpin him financially. Henry's capacity to keep in with rivals Cecil and Dudley, without apparently incurring the mistrust of either, was a singular factor in his advancement.

One of Henry's achievements on this short and dangerous mission to France followed the sudden death of the French king. He escaped through the French information blockade, journeying from Paris to Greenwich in twenty-four hours to deliver the news - a fact noted with admiration by her Majesty and perhaps remembered by a string of unhappy horses. A few years later unfavourable winds and a shortage of French horses extended one of Killigrew's journeys on this route to eleven days.

Germany, France, now Scotland! The weakening of France through internal division presented the English with an incentive to weaken Gallic influence north of the border - by supporting Scottish Protestants, preventing the arrival of French military help and securing the removal of French troops based in Scotland. Spies skilled in subversion and preferably with Protestant credentials were urgently needed. Perhaps a Celtic background would also be helpful. The tireless Henry was finding his talents much in demand. Like Throckmorton he was becoming highly effective at combining respectable diplomacy with undercover espionage.

In 1560 Harry toiled northwards. As before he discovered that Elizabeth was less alert to bring things to a successful conclusion than he felt was necessary. English support of Scottish Protestants was inadequate and led to reversals for which Killigrew unfairly received some blame. However, events conspired against the French and by 1561 their power was seriously reduced in Scotland, for which Harry earned some credit.

At home he had little scope for religious campaigning, but worked with elder brother John, heir apparent at Arwennack, to obtain for militant protestant William Ramsay the church living of Tiverton in Devon.

Already he was jeopardising his political position for his ideal, although this may not have been obvious to him at the time. Elizabethan England had no concept of a loyal opposition or even coherent factions, although lobbies might exist on specific matters. If you sought to challenge royal opinion you risked being branded as a self-seeking individualist, lurking in the darkness clutching your greed: perhaps a traitor!

For the moment Killigrew judged his opponents well. A crucial advancement in his career was propelled by Cecil, who no doubt recognised the need to pay Henry properly for his work (all diplomatic work was notoriously badly rewarded and involved substantial expense to the individual). Killigrew was appointed as one of four who held the important and remunerative office of Teller of the Exchequer. This was not a sinecure, but vital to the state, requiring considerable skill and attention to detail. The award of this office signalled that Henry's talents were needed at home as well as abroad, and that he had been accepted by the cautious as well as by the radicals and Marian exiles.

Cecil also controlled the distribution of lucrative wardships, and Henry came by valuable further income when he assumed responsibility for the young Cornishman John Arundell of Gwernecke, heir to Trerice.

Perhaps Henry's appointment as a Gentleman of the Privy Chamber occurred at this time. This was an important if un-feed Court office, bringing highly trusted and well regarded people considerably closer to the Queen as they stood in readiness to receive and transmit the most personal of royal errands. Attendance at Court in the royal apartments was a regular duty, bringing considerable honour. Other Gentlemen included Sir Christopher Hatton and Fulke Greville.

In 1560 Harry lived for a time at the Court and at some point around then he seems to have given way, rather reassuringly it may be felt, to a little human weakness. His bastard son, Harry Caltropt, was born a year later. Who was the mother? Given the vagaries of contemporary spelling, were there connections with Charles Calthorpe, associate of Leicester and Cecil, who entered Parliament in 1572 through the patronage of Bacon and became Attorney General in Ireland many years later? Did the Cooke family - through Ann Bacon perhaps - get to hear about the making of this little Harry?

Around now Killigrew acquired his house in St Paul's Churchyard, close to the famous open air pulpit. He was in situ by 1561, but left it for a while in 1562 when he visited Cornwall, travelling as far as St Michael's Mount.

It would be very much better if this courtier - with his experience in office, steady income, reputation as an upright religious radical, position at Court, nice house and proven fertility - were to find a suitably protestant wife to help him found his own dynasty. There was even one of the Cooke sisters unaccounted for, who would bring instant access to her important relations.

In spite of progress in Scotland, the overall European situation still remained unhopeful for radical protestants: spiritually and intellectually Henry must have been jarred by impatience. This conflict would rear up in the following year during some soldiering at Rouen.

DEATH ON
THE RIVER SEINE.

When Henry Killigrew was thirty five he was chosen to guide England right at the front line of its latest confrontation with France.

He must have recognised that the demands of this assignment would test not only the sharpness of his professional skills but also the depth of his principles and the strength of his physical courage. Along the sky-line he saw his own high standards for which he might have to put his life at risk.

As he rode down the track from London to the ship awaiting him at the Channel port on that July day in 1562, many of Harry's talents were loaded around him. His experience of soldiering, knowledge of French politics, expertise in handling money, proven diplomatic ability, even perhaps his association with Cornish pirates, above all his religious convictions.

Henry carried with him 3,000 crowns from the English Government for revictualling the Protestant garrison at Havre. On 30th July he arrived at the quay at Havre and reported to the town's governor.

Havre, Dieppe and Rouen in the north of France were controlled by Frenchmen in open rebellion against their Catholic dominated Government. These towns had been well chosen by the rebels: they dominated the main supply line to Paris and could starve central France too: they were now hard pressed and had asked for assistance from Queen Elizabeth of England.

The leaders of Havre probably knew that Henry was also a spy. His role as an English agent for over ten years had already brought him into contact with the town's governor. Henry's real task was to advise his own Government on whether they should send more help or abandon the Huguenots as a lost cause. Cecil had determined to send a 'skilful man-of-war' to test the strength of Protestant resistance in Havre and Dieppe.

Were the garrisons well fortified? How many soldiers were under arms? What was the morale of these men, townspeople and destitute refugees from other parts of France? Were powerful voices in the town sounding against resistance to the French Government? Would the towns accept English reinforcements or would prejudice against these hold greater sway?

Henry advised Cecil, in a letter on 10th August, that the Huguenots could not prevail without English help - in numbers which he estimated - and assistance would be acceptable to soldiers and the population. However, Huguenot leaders were dithering.

Killigrew understood the terrible search they were making for the lesser of evils, for to invite in the old enemy from England would call down on their heads the wrath of a multitude of Frenchmen. They knew Elizabeth of England would not be sending soldiers out of profound religious commitment (for she had none), but - spurred on by Dudley - she hoped to regain English jurisdiction over Calais. She was also hoping that Protestant ascendancy in France would prevent French and Spanish collaboration against her.

If she intervened in France, the young Queen, now four years on the throne, would be taking risks herself. Should she fail Calais might be lost for ever, and she would have revealed herself as openly and actively hostile to these European powers still firmly in the ascendent. There were still many Catholics in her own realm whose loyalty to her had not been put to the test.

Not for the first or last time Henry found himself alone in a foreign land forcing unpalatable English truths down people's throats. Polite diplomacy fell away as he drilled into the French the reality of their predicament and hastened their irrevocable decision to ask for help. Once this job was completed among local Huguenot leaders - but not unfortunately their national ones - Harry was convinced his presence in Havre was stirring up anti-English feeling which should be stifled for the time being. He set off by boat to Dieppe en route for home.

On this short north easterly sea journey along the French coast Harry's boat encountered a ferocious August storm. To save themselves, he and other passengers were forced to throw their baggage overboard. It was also necessary to jettison the mast whose weight under pressure from the wind was endangering the boat. When they reached Dieppe the storm had still not abated. This town does not enjoy the broad entrance and wide area of shelter afforded by the Fal roadstead. On entering the harbour the boat nearly capsized and the passengers almost drowned. Writing the following day in dry clothes from his lodgings, Harry informed the Principal Secretary 'I was never in danger before the like to be compared'.

When Henry returned to London a week or so later to report to the Government, Dudley and other key players, he probably knew he had not seen the last of Havre and Dieppe. He had been chosen for this mission in part for his rapport with Huguenot leaders, which in turn was based on his known Protestant sympathies. He would not wish to be left out of the coming engagement and would continue to be a useful intermediary.

Dudley had to persuade Cecil and Elizabeth to confirm the English offer of 6,000 men to garrison Havre and a provide a million crowns on loan. Reports of further hostility to the English from some Protestant leaders elsewhere in France cast doubt on whether the English fleet, now ready to sail from Portsmouth, would be allowed to land its army. Elizabeth, to limit possible damage to relations with France, restricted her forthcoming role in France to defence of Dieppe and Havre, and forbade her army to advance the fifty miles up the River Seine to relieve Rouen. These limitations may have soothed some Huguenots' fears, but left others feeling betrayed.

Killigrew probably spent September actively drumming up support in London for the Huguenot cause. He also provisioned himself with five light horsemen to transport across the Channel, whose equipment and wages were paid out of his own resources. Perhaps he thought this was an honourable way to spend wealth acquired during the disposal of monastic property in Truro.

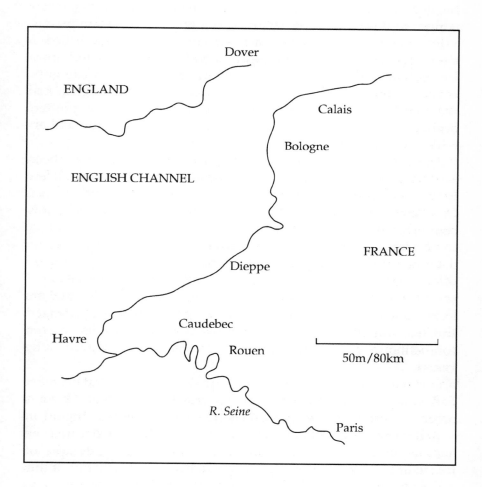

At the end of September the national Huguenot leaders were again saying 'no English'. Cecil asked Killigrew to make a secret journey to Havre to ascertain whether the local leaders would defy the wider leadership and admit the English. Accompanied by his private cavalry the Christian Soldier set off on the first stage of a journey which would bring him great physical injury and a spell in prison.

French Catholics were now actively counter-attacking. If Rouen fell to their siege they would descend on Channel ports and finish off resistance there. Panic was setting in at Havre, and Killigrew himself was besieged for explanations as to why the English had not come. He busied himself uncomfortably with writing letters urging the English to sail, and with finding lodgings for the soldiers whom he believed were on their way.

Those days watching out for the English fleet must also have been a time of reflection for Henry. He could choose the comparative safety of the town, a few steps from the line of retreat to England by boat. Or he could freelance with his little troupe into the battle field now being prepared, and risk his life.

All Henry's experience predisposed him to fight. He was no disturbed mercenary eager for the first opportunity to enjoy the blood of battle. In his world view, shared by many others, the Devil loitered among enemy forces, seeking every English weakness. Evil powers locked in the assault on God's earthly kingdom must be challenged and overcome. This was not a matter of rival dynasties or even competing religious emphases, but a cosmic battle which must be joined.

On the arrival of the English in Havre Henry poured out his relief and enthusiasm in a letter to Cecil. His frustration with his Queen's procrastinations was evident. "The Queen's Majesty is bound in honour, a penny spent now will save three. God prosper you as he has begun, and inspire her Majesty to build up the temple of Jeruselum... it lieth within her power to banish idolatry out of this realm'. He added ruefully, 'You will think me over holy for a soldier'.

Cecil however was no doubt familiar with the clarity of Harry's glowing ideals.

The Huguenots were now preparing to send a party from Havre to relieve Rouen, and urged the English to join them. The English commander - Dudley's brother - was under orders from Elizabeth not to do so. Although the reign was still young the Queen had a reputation for dealing with disobedience.

The stakes of Henry's career as a disciplined diplomat were on the table. In the previous four years since Elizabeth came to the throne, Henry's reputation had been built on capacity to deal in caution and diplomatic ambiguities. It is not difficult to envisage the temptation to trim his views to those of the Queen.

It was not to be so. What demons, ghosts and gargoyles Henry wrestled with in Havre we do not know, but on 8th October 200 English soldiers under Leighton and a similar number of French under Killigrew's own leadership were ordered by the English commander to set off up river in boats. Old Cornish pirate Henry Strangeways provided navigation: this long-standing friend and accomplice of Henry's brothers in their activities out of Arwennack had been released from prison to aid the enterprise in France.

Up to this point everything had developed as Harry wished. The Queen had committed money and troops to support his cherished Protestant cause, albeit in a limited way, the fleet had avoided summer storms, Huguenots had accepted English on their soil, the English commander had been persuaded to go into action over the head of his Sovereign, and Harry had been given part of that work. He must have prayed that his five horsemen could ride out any river-sickness.

Everything now depended on the outcome of the fighting. Although he was a small man, who would be discerned only with difficulty by a short-sighted attacker, Hal would have needed protection. The armour he wore may have survived from his soldiering during his exile, or been allocated during training on the Dudley's lawns at Ely Place, or fallen out of a corner at Arwennack after surviving as a relic of bellicose Celtic ancestors.

The fifty-mile journey up the Seine from Havre to Rouen begins on a broad estuary and then modulates to a wide and winding river. Most of the countryside on the banks lay with French Catholics who were unlikely to stand and admire the skills of Strangeway's navigation. However Catholics held their fire until the twin forces were deeply committed, only eighteen miles from Rouen at

Caudebec.

The Catholics apparently lacked powerful ordnance but had staked the river to force the boats to pass within range of gunshot. Killigrew and some Huguenot soldiers in one of the first boats were among those who edged through, but many others were killed or wounded and captured. Strangeways although shot managed to continue but died further up river. The captured English were hanged from a tree on orders from brutal French leader Montmorency, old enemy of Harry's.

Killigrew, still sure no doubt that God was on his side, pressed on to Rouen. He achieved entry but found the town on its last legs. The defences had begun to fall to Catholic besiegers firing down onto the garrison, which was about to surrender. Only Leighton's English were adequately furnished with pikes and they fought vigorously, shuttling from one section of the walls to another in the hope of exaggerating their numbers.

On 26th October, twelve days after Harry left Havre, the decisive battle occurred. The third Catholic assault on the town finally broke down the resistance of the English, who were located in the forefront of defence, and many were killed at their posts. Eighty wounded English survivors had their throats slit and their bodies stripped and thrown into the Seine.

Amos Miller completes the story. 'Killigrew had been shot in the foot by an arquebus during the first assault, and when Rouen fell on the same day, he was lying in a lodging within the town with a Huguenot officer who had both legs blown off. This was a moment of fear and mortal danger for Killigrew. Rouen was now filled with drunken riotous soldiers of the victorious army who threw themselves wholeheartedly into an orgy of looting, murder, burning and rape... they were especially eager to find any Englishmen whose throats had not been cut.

'Disabled by his wound Killigrew could neither defend himself nor attempt to escape, and he was soon discovered by Captain Causin, a gentleman of the horse to the Duke de Longueville. Probably only the fact that Killigrew was an officer and a man of some station kept his captor from despatching him on the spot.. Causin had him placed in the Castle of Rouen - where Joan of Arc had been imprisoned before her execution in 1431. There he found himself in the company of Thomas Leighton who had also been taken prisoner when the town fell'.

Henry now found himself prisoner. Castles must have figured in his childhood fantasies, but Pendennis cannot have been more scary than the castle at Rouen.

How do you explain defeat when you have fought your best for God? Unequal odds can scarcely be an adequate excuse, for did not David slay Goliath? As defeat crashed round him, was Henry now assailed with doubts about the correctness of seeking to relieve Rouen without the Queen's official sanction? Was he being punished for his own sin? Had he like others in his family allowed himself to cross the line from legitimate privateering to piracy? Or could he fall back on the convenient excuse of the Evil Counsellor? Was he dismayed by the lack of spirit of French Huguenot leaders and soldiers?

Soon after his capture and still in great pain, Harry was taken on horse-back from the castle to be interviewed by the French Catholic leaders. His mind may have been elsewhere: it was likely his shattered foot would need amputating - an operation which would probably kill him. Although they thought he had been acting with the Queen's unofficial sanction, the French claimed to regard him as proceeding without orders, and hence worthy of death rather than protection under rules of war. However Montmorency's son stepped in to ensure his safety, loyal perhaps to friends they shared - and hoping for ransom.

Henry was taken to another castle in the country north of Paris where he was closely confined for six months. His wound was allowed to heal, while negotiations for his release were conducted.

When he heard about the capture and imprisonment, Cecil sought to find out about Killigrew's condition. Harry's younger brother William, who was not yet a Court official, was sent over the Havre to make enquiries. Meanwhile people at Court, with the callousness of the age, began to bid for Henry's lucrative post as Teller. In their eyes he had failed in his enterprise, surely the indication of a guilty soul?

This smaller bastion where Killigrew was imprisoned may have been the still in which were condensed the guiding principles which spirited the rest of his life.

Although he later wrote a number of memoirs of his life he rarely indicates the state of his feelings. This reflects the muted sense of self in Tudor times, even among Calvinists. Self-fashioning belonged to God, whose Divine Grace dictated the individual's fate. We can only infer from later actions how he responded to events. This man with a promising career had given way to frustration and abandoned his normal caution. The subsequent endeavour had resulted in the failure of his cause, death of friends and serious personal injury. He had shown himself unreliable in a major way.

A study of his life suggests that following his return to England in May 1562 Henry spent ten years involved with increasingly radical and militant operations against Catholic powers, espousing all the techniques of Tudor terror including unlawful killing. Clearly he bounced back from his reversal using the psychology of the extremist: not himself but the Divine Enemy was to blame. *More* energy was required to defeat the demons.

Prison stiffened his resolve, but we can reasonably assume that he must have searched every niche of his soul's castle. In those times a man of thirty five years old was lodging on the threshold of middle age. He must have sat in pain, waiting for the next visit of the physician, and remembered his earlier wounds sustained in childhood and adolescence: also friends' broken bones, his brothers' enemies left bruised and bleeding, agonised horses damaged beyond repair in Dudley's fields?

Another question must have raged. At home now were children being freshly made, young Cecils and Throckmortons, Hobys and Bacons, while no laughter of women rang through the cold castle walls? And what did Catherine hear of him? Could he hear her prayers?

Many hands were working for his release. The Queen read Throckmorton's account of Harry's bravery at Rouen and heard Dudley's arguments in his defence. She was uncharacteristically willing to accept that her over-caution had contributed to the defeat. Meanwhile Harry's brother continued to negotiate terms for his release. Dudley wrote to the French, and Maitland, a leader of the

Scottish Protestants, induced Mary Queen of Scots to send a letter on Killigrew's behalf to her Catholic Royal kin in France.

Eventually Harry bought himself out, putting to further good use the fruits of his Cornish estates and other revenues. In gratitude for his release he wrote a poem, which has not survived, to present to Maitland.

In later years Henry looked back on this episode with pride. It had not been a success politically, but he had proved his own valour to others, and mostly importantly, to himself. Like Ralegh later, he had acquired a limp as an insignia to stimulate others' memories of his days of action.

MID LIFE OASIS.

We do not know much about Catherine. She exchanged letters with the scholarly religious radical Dering, she suffered poor health in later life and sometimes wrote poetry. Mysteriously these achievements earned her a place in the Dictionary of National Biography.

The last of the Cooke daughters to marry! The decision of her life which tells us most about her is that she surveyed the wide field of possible partners and selected Harry Killigrew.

It must have been quite a wedding at St Peter le Poor in London. November 4th 1565 is the date which has come down to us. Catherine's day... and did it not belong a little to Sir Antony Cooke?

Cooke must by now have become famous for the success with which he had trained up his daughters in New Learning and new politics. Happy enough now, old man, living in his grand house of Gidea Park in Essex, enjoying his books and notions of Jerusalem, he had never been very interested in occupying high office. The troubles of power could be left to the in-laws from London, dour friendless William Cecil, most prominent statesman in the land, and clever Chancellor Nicholas Bacon, versatile Thomas Hoby, writer, translator and latest Ambassador to France.

Did the Cornish relations at these nuptials include Sir John and his sea-faring sons, Dame Margaret Godolphin and the shadowy debt-ridden blustering Trewynnards?

Did all the sisters turn out on that day? Mildred Cecil, whose quiet severity stands out from her portrait, respected in later years by as good a judge as Ralegh? Ann Bacon, who in her eccentric and angry widowhood became a courageous reformist campaigner? Elizabeth Hoby, whose drawing by Holbein gives a hint of her reputation as the most awkward sister, and who faced down King James when she was seventy eight?

Did the smaller guests included two whose genius infused the next generation, Robert Cecil, one day to take over the psychopathology of power from his father, and Francis Bacon, less successful as a politician but just as unlovable, whose writings are studied to this day?

Where, the tactless among them might have asked Catherine, did little Hal fit into all this? With his Genevan ideas and his strange ability to get on with the Scots - both characteristics so un-English - and his limp, and all those Cornish relations?

We were made for each other, she may have said (a Calvinist belief in predestination is handy). He is a coming man, he will be a Principal Secretary one day soon (with a little help from the rest of you), he writes well, and Cornwall is a very long distance from here, they don't get up very often, and Sir John Killigrew is very busy rebuilding his house.

Catherine must have been ready for marriage. Like sister Elizabeth, she was thirty before her wedding. It was probably a marriage of love, from her side at least there would have been nobler or richer suitors to choose from among the devout. It helped that they shared those religious convictions located well towards the margins of orthodoxy.

Harry had been prepared to fight for his bride. Cecil records that on Easter Day 1564 'H. Killigrew wrote me an invective for my misliking of his marriage with my sister, Cooke'. Catherine had been spending some time with the Cecils so William knew her well, but his misliking of Harry is more likely to be political than personal. Either way, it was a brave letter.

Cecil was a snob: coming like Henry from middle ranking gentry, he would have liked Catherine to mix it with the aristocracy. More strongly it was a question of real power. Family networks were important in underpinning factions at Court. Sometimes things went wrong - there was a serious breach between Cecil and Bacon around then - so you should not take chances. Cecil was vulnerable to his main rival Dudley, who often had better access to the Queen's ear (and other parts too apparently) and who had now been created Earl of Leicester. Harry was one of Dudley's men - and Cecil would go on saying this to people after the wedding. Cecil could have found a dozen people in his own network whom he would have liked to bind into the family.

In addition, there were genuine and fundamental differences between Cecil and Killigrew. Cecil believed in religious moderation not only for political expediency but as an Erasmian ideal. Religious change should come from the top and maintain the integration of church and state. Henry's Calvinist presbyterianism was a response to energies emerging closer to the clergy and congregations.

Sir Anthony Cooke is likely to have approved of Henry. Although his own religious convictions were softening in old age he would have admired the fire of the young, and cared less about Cecil's factions. In any event he had probably learnt to let his daughters hang their own tapestries of the heart and probably all others too, particularly daughter Elizabeth's tapestries.

The Queen was no doubt consulted, certainly if Henry was already a Gentleman of the Privy Chamber. It was normally only the men whom she fancied, or fancied she fancied, whose marriages she objected to. Poor Dudley and Ralegh and Essex.

Once the pair were married, Killigrew's connections and ability meant that Cecil had to take him seriously and treat the new brother-in-law as an asset rather than a Trojan horse for Leicester.

The marriage provided considerable advantages for Harry's career. When he joined the gilded circle, others would have an interest in promoting him. That calculation cannot have figured too strongly though. Later evidence shows that he was devoted to Catherine. Many Tudor marriages although possessing clear political advantages to either party demonstrated much mutual fondness, if not initially then in due course - the well documented marriage between Arthur Lisle and Honor Basset providing an example.

Killigrew maintained his stand on religion, and moved things forward when he could, but career was not everything to him. It seems quite likely that as the decade progressed he became less interested in the highest office- certainly overseas - if indeed he ever had been. Diplomacy was financially unrewarding, and increasingly he probably shared Walsingham's distaste for the tackier aspects of it. He was no doubt concerned to guard his back and safeguard the position he had already achieved. Paradoxically his disinterest in power may have increased his attractiveness as a diplomat in the eyes of the Queen and Cecil.

As the historian MacCaffrey wrote, at this time the English diplomatic service was 'still embryonic in form... its permanent establishment consisted of a Paris embassy regularly maintained, an Edinburgh mission only spasmodically staffed since the Darnley marriage, a few floating diplomats, most notably Henry Killigrew and Thomas Randolph, and a half forgotten ambassador in Madrid'.

His work in the Exchequer may have clinked more to his liking. As he moved into his forties he seems to have developed the side of his personality neglected by militarism and protestant diplomacy, the interests of a member of the rural gentry. He may have looked with some envy at the life of his brother in law Sir Francis Godolphin. Yet, when opportunities arose to accept assignments where he could promote radical religion, he did not stint to accept them.

Henry must have been distressed by the death of his former travelling companion and brother in law Thomas Hoby, Ambassador in France. The Queen's reaction is interesting: the fulsomeness of her letter to the widow Elizabeth suggests that she felt her namesake was a kindred spirit. 'We hear out of France such singular good reports of your duty well accomplished towards your husband, both living and dead, with other your sober, wise and discreet behaviour in that Court and Country, that we think it a part of great contentation to us, and commendation of our Country, that such a Gentlewoman hath given so manifest a testimony of virtue in such hard times of adversity. And therefore though we thought very well of you before, yet shall we hereafter make a more assured account of your virtues and gifts, and wherein soever we may conveniantly do you pleasure, you may be thereof assured. And so we would have you to rest yourself in quietness, with a firm opinion of our especiall favour towards you'. There was Elizabeth at her best, nurturing the devotion of subjects.

After his release from the French prison in 1563 and before he married, Henry had spent nearly three years at home, with the exception of a brief mission to France. He had concentrated on his personal life and his important work in the Exchequer. He was elected member of parliament for Saltash in 1563, no doubt attending its sittings from January to April.

In 1566 it was becoming obvious that his role as a diplomat and secret agent was going to be needed again.

To Scotland again! Henry made two trips in that year with a young secretary Davison. The politics in that country were a constantly shifting kaleidoscope whose patterns were built from a basis of different clans and religious factions. Some wanted England as a friend, others wanted France.

The sovereign was Mary Stuart (Queen of Scots) who possessed little political judgment but considerable courage. Also an extraordinary charm which she used to implicate a succession of men in her affairs, rarely to their advantage: even the psychologically sturdy Nicholas Throckmorton had been smitten. Hal displaced any attraction he might have felt into manoeuvring her, with all the thrusting energy that was required, towards a righteous Catholic death. To those sharing his view, Mary was the epitome of the Devil's agent as she schemed against Elizabeth, England and Protestantism.

England must at very least prevent the Scots from joining with foreign powers to work against English interests. At best England and Scotland might form a mutually advantageous alliance. Many in England already envisaged a union between the two independent states, either based on an immediate dynastic marriage or by virtue of a Stuart succeeding Elizabeth on the English throne.

Henry arrived in Edinburgh to convey Elizabeth's displeasure at Scottish meddling in Ireland. He was the first Englishmen to see Mary's new-born son, who later became the less than fully admirable King James the First of England. Killigrew already understood that Scottish politics were in crisis. Mary had recently almost lost her throne in a rebellion by her husband and others against her Italian favourite. He also noted the growing role of a third of Mary's intimates, the sinister Bothwell. Henry sized up the situation and journeyed to London to report.

Killigrew was glad to return to the rim of the glittering circle. In

1566 he wrote to his new cousin by marriage, Hugh Fitzwilliam, giving a vivid account of one of the extended pageants mounted by Leicester for the Queen at Kenilworth Castle: 'My Lady Fitzwilliam was there and said she would never look to see the like in her days. Twenty oxen at breakfast was nothing. Speak it upon my credit.'

Henry's credit! That was certainly growing in those days. The four Tellers received all the revenues paid into the Exchequer, often through bureaux maintained at the Queen's expense in their own houses, where the money was stored in strong boxes. They were only required to submit half-yearly accounts and meanwhile could use the accumulating sums for short term loans: although this practice was illegal it was widely used by people in government circles, and Harry appears to have benefitted from the system in this way.

It was the Teller's job to pay ambassadors and envoys. Henry seems have been scrupulous in this role, even penny pinching. One such ambassador was Killigrew's old friend Thomas Randolph who in 1566 was resident in Scotland. He wrote to Cecil: "I pray you to charge Harry Killigrew who is harder unto me than ever Browne the Treasurer was". This tactic was counter-productive and later he felt obliged to apologise to Cecil for his 'doing touching Mr Killigrew'.

The 1563 parliament sat again for three months at the end of 1566.

You never get anything for nothing in this world, especially if you get on well with the Scots. A year later, in March 1567, Harry was again torn from his family to make the wearisome journey northwards on horseback into the persisting Scottish winter. He may have looked forward to renewing acquaintance with valued presbyterian confederates but his mission was tricky. A few weeks earlier loathesome Mary's husband had been murdered by Bothwell, and she was being accused of complicity.

Elizabeth wanted Mary to clear her name: this was one of the first of many examples of Elizabeth's sympathy and forebearance - many felt weak-headedness - towards the eel-like Mary which later endangered her own life. Elizabeth briefed Henry personally: as he wrote later, he 'had no other instructions than from her Majesty's own mouth, but they were so loving and kind that her (Mary's) natural mother, I think, if she had then been alive could have shown no more sorrow for her estate nor care to preserve her honour than her Majesty did'.

Harry went to Holyrood Palace in Edinburgh and met Mary in a dramatically darkened room in which he could barely make out her features. She seemed grateful for Elizabeth's letter and grief-stricken about her husband, and promised to put Bothwell on trial.

Harry's memorandum shows signs of rapid dictation: 'if she had followed in effect as she had promised to have done, I believe verily that she had not fallen into the great calamity that since befell her in neglecting so wise and princely counsel, for had she dealt bona fide in bringing the Earl of Bothwell to his trial, who was the suspected murderer of her husband, which was her advice she should do to any whomsoever in Scotland, the sequel had not, in all likelihood, happened to her that had done since...'

As before he returned to England after only a brief visit. In later years he would revisit Scotland and be less fortunate over the duration of his stay.

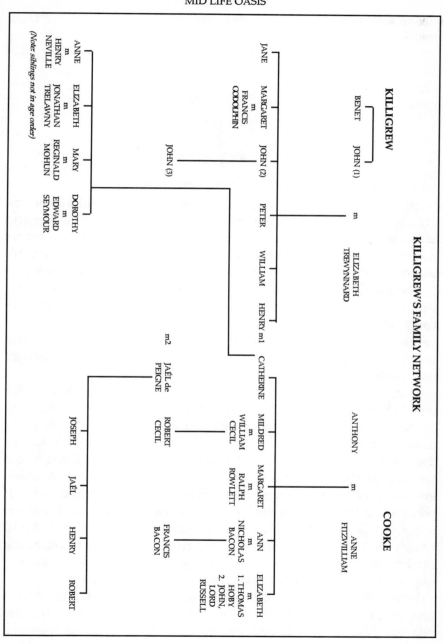

KILLIGREW'S FAMILY NETWORK

A LARGER WIND.

At the end of 1568 Philip of Spain noted England's intention to push the Spanish military off the English doorstep and take further steps towards becoming a world power. He was not pleased, and because he was free for a while from his greater pre-occupation with Turks, he found himself in a position to act.

The main theatre of conflict for the following twenty years was the Netherlands. Other front lines were Cornwall and the new trade-route into Germany.

During that winter Henry lived for a while in Cornwall and watched the movement of Spanish ships. Then he sailed to Hamburg and Heidelberg.

Cornwall was a stressful place to live in the second half of the sixteenth century, not only for vulnerable prawns in the waters and for rabbits among foxes and stoats on the moors. If you looked out to sea you would muse that Spain might attack from the south or the north - perhaps via Ireland. If you looked westward you might wonder at the New World slowly opening up to unpredictable energies, where no Pope or monarch or preacher imposed order. If you looked upward you might consider the many shifts of religion and try to guess which of the clouds concealed the face of God and which the Devil. If you looked to the ground you might note rising poverty and unrest. Look inward and you may see the dull canvas of predestined fate and all the cameos of remembered sin.

While Henry and Catherine were visiting their family and properties in Cornwall the trouble with Spain began to disturb the peace. Killigrew's father had recently died, having just completed a considerable extension and rebuilding of Arwennack, so that it was now revealed as one of the finest houses in the county. His elder brother John was now in possession of the house and Killigrew lands around the Fal, and had also replaced old Sir John as governor of Pendennis. Henry apparently had no house in Cornwall, and probably divided his time between visiting his brother at Arwennack, his sister who was mistress at Godolphin, and the Trelawnys at Poole in Menheniot whose heir was his ward.

He may not have been surprised that John immediately followed his father's stratagems in bending the law. This behaviour was not personal aberration but part of a way of life which served the purposes of many in that century including the highest in the land. But magpies fall out: former member of parliament Uncle James Trewynnard in that year entered one of his nephew's properties at Killifreth in Kenwyn and carried off 100 gallons of black tin.

Apart from Killigrew good neighbourliness, all was quiet above the water line until the Spanish ships arrived. Sir Francis Godolphin in particular was doing his best to make up for the absence in Cornwall of an aristocratic culture of big houses with their pageants and music, plays and players. The gentry made their own culture, as Carnsew's diary shows us: they were well informed and read widely, exchanging the latest books as readily as they swopped horses.

The house on the Fal was maintained as a gentleman's residence, even if it also operated as a control centre for a sea-borne and inland mafia. It had become a focus for ecclesiastical administration, thereby demonstrating the strong hold which the gentry maintained over the church at this time. Into this house in 1566 and again in 1569 the Bishop of Exeter descended to conduct ordinations: not all those ordained passed their subsequent performance reviews.

Even before the Spanish trouble began to foam in the West, there was brabble in London. The fading elite of ancient nobles such as the Duke of Norfolk, including some with Catholic sympathies, were joining forces with political opportunists to resist the growing ascendancy in Government of Protestant gentry and members of the trading community. If Cecil was the first in their sights, Walsingham, Killigrew and others would rapidly follow. The traditionalists strongly disliked antagonising Spain and wanted the Scottish Catholic Queen Mary, now sheltering in England from political failure north of the border, to be named as Elizabeth's successor. Many of them were in touch with the French and Spanish, seeking for allies to help them impose their will on the Queen.

For a while Elizabeth and Cecil were thrust back into deep defence, and there could only be one victorious side. The lengthy conflict did not turn out to be an amiable affair. After a major rebellion failed Cecil and Walsingham seem to have set up the vulnerable Italian Ridolphi to catch as many as possible in a bogus plot. When Norfolk failed to fall deeply enough into the hole dug for him, the evidence of his guilt was apparently fabricated by Cecil, and his noble head fell into the basket.

It is unlikely that Killigrew was not involved with Cecil and Walsingham in this extraordinary and complex intrigue. The Ridolphi episode shows that the violence of the early Tudor period could return at any time if a few strong individuals lost their judgment. Sides were taken in bitterness and even if foreign powers were not branded as satanic the enemy at home was draped in demonic vestments.

As Smith comments: "what gave to Tudor treason its fascination and diabolic quality was not its frequency but its urgency and potency... struggles for good and evil might bring about the collapse of kingdoms, the traitor stood as a kind of Judas, driven by evil but the only instrument through which God and providential change could operate".

This was Cecil's closest shave. He had said how sorry he was for poor Norfolk and, while things were still hanging in the balance for the aristocrat, William had tried to marry him off to Hoby's abrasive widow Elizabeth. That would have made Cecil and Norfolk brothers. Cecil's most cynical act of political match-making, one historian has commented.

Such affairs often brew up in the atmosphere of paranoia engendered by the threat of enemies peering at you from over the water. As the Cornish gentry understood - or Henry Killigrew could have told them - the threat of Spain, which had been muted since the Queen came to the throne, now burst into a fanfare. Up to this point the English had been more directly troubled by France, and had been glad of Spain's calculated balancing of power. France was now drastically weakened by internal divisions, and the King of Spain no longer needed to fear French reprisals if he sought to encircle them and become the indisputably dominant power. Also Philip no longer had to hold back from squeezing England in case that action drove her into the hands of the French.

The new era of confrontation had sown its seeds in the Spanish Netherlands in 1567 when Philip - freed for a while from anxiety about the Turks in the Mediterranean - sent a tough and effective commander, Alva, to suppress political and religious rebellion. Philip was in many ways a more civilised and humane character than he has been pictured, and his Catholicism was based on devotion and sincerity as well as political expansionism. Yet he was a fanatical anti-Protestant, who was determined to use his New World silver to suppress Calvinists every time they appeared from behind their prayer books.

Spanish policy set off few favourable altar gongs in England, apart from among a few increasingly prostrate Catholic traditionalists. There was widespread conviction that if Philip were allowed to bring the Netherlands into line and leave his soldiers there he would then find an excuse to intervene and colonise England. Garrisoning of soldiers in the Netherlands was the big issue for many years to come. Other matters - protection of England's trade through Antwerp and in the New World - were important but unlikely to lead either side to war.

Cecil, although surely immune by now to Killigrew's bellicosity, was coming round to the view that the English should at least intervene to undermine a rival's strength in the Netherlands, as they had done in France and Scotland. This meant alliances with German Princes and Protestant monarchs in Sweden and Denmark. This minimalist view was based on a recognition that England did not possess the army, navy or finances for open conflict. The Queen - with her strategic genius and mistrust of ideals - would also take much persuading. She did not want a vacuum in the Netherlands in case the French marched in, so Spain could rule the Netherlands as harshly as it wished, and impose Catholicism to its heart's content, as long as the troops were withdrawn.

Although the Netherlands were the issue, the New World was the trigger. Things came dramatically to a head during that winter when Henry was in Cornwall.

The English had been slow to follow the Spanish, Portuguese and, to a lesser extent, the French in developing colonies and trade beyond Europe. There had been little pressure to do so, as their need for overseas trade was largely satisfied by commerce in wool and finished cloth through Antwerp. Now however, Elizabethans were becoming more active.

John Hawkins of Plymouth, a member of the second of three great generations of that family and a peaceful sailor with good intentions towards Spain, decided to trade in African slaves: slave labour was sorely needed by those Spanish American colonists who had ravaged and depleted their native populations. John had returned from his first three-cornered trip of 1562-3 with a cargo of gold, silver, pearls, hides and sugar, and understood that the Spanish in the New World were not concerned to defend a monopoly of trade in the region which had been declared from the Spanish mainland.

In planning a second trip Hawkins had obtained the patronage of the Queen, Dudley and Cecil. Perhaps Harry Killigrew was a party to these negotiations, although he does not seem to have invested money. Philip now forbade his colonies to admit the English, so Hawkins prepared defiance, armed himself and conducted a successful second trip which rewarded its shareholders.

A third trip, under Elizabeth's flag and with Drake in command of Judith, set off in 1567, with the Spanish now on high alert. After a troublesome journey to Africa and across the Atlantic, on 20th September 1568 Hawkins and Drake put into the port of San Juan de Ulloa in Mexico. Here Spaniards used treachery to come alongside and attack the English. A number of English ships and part of the treasure were lost, the other boats escaped.

In December while these ships were limping home, rumour preceded them to Plymouth claiming that John Hawkins had been killed. At this point a fleet of Spanish ships, laden with £400,000 of treasure, was driven into the small Cornish ports of Fowey and Saltash by French pirates. This money was intended to pay Alva's troops for their hostile activities in the Netherlands.

That most respectable of Plymouth citizens, Hawkins' elder brother William, wrote to Cecil suggesting that this treasure should be impounded. As Rowse put it, Cecil 'hardly needed the suggestion', but he needed operators grounded in treachery and guile. He sent letters to the West Country ordering his trusty instruments John Killigrew (who was after all a category of brother) and Henry Champernowne 'under colour of friendship' to acquire the treasure for the Queen. Duly professing friendship to the Spanish, and pointing out how the English were waiting to advise them when the coast was clear of pirates, Harry's brother and his friend supervised the Spaniards in the emptying out of their own cargo and wrote careful receipts before the money was sealed and stored under their trusting eyes.

The Spanish government was not so gullible and set an embargo on all English shipping, which was immediately reciprocated. Spanish ships stayed in the West Country were estimated at £40,000. Anchored in the Fal, perhaps under the eyes of the visiting Henry and Catherine, was 'a Flemish hulk of 140 tons, laden with sugar, molasses, canary wine, and 5000 odd reals of plate; a Spaniard of 80 tons laden with figs, and a Portuguese of 50 tons laden with sugar and some silver plate'. How John Killigrew's fingers must have caressed the lids of those holds.

At the end of January, in the middle of this confrontation, John Hawkins arrived in Mountsbay (westward of the Fal) and Drake dragged himself to Plymouth. Many men were dead, the rest starving, and the ships in serious disrepair. News of Spanish treachery at San Juan spread out across the West Country and up to London. The Spanish treasure also found its way under guard to London and steps were taken to prepare Cornwall for Spanish reprisals. At Pendennis John Killigrew lined up a gun 'complete with slivers of brass', two culverins, two demi-culverins, two sacres, with powder and shot, a quantity of bows and arrows, bills and pikes.

Young men, some of Henry's timbre fired with zeal, others greedy for booty, glided over to France to fight with the Huguenots, still in revolt against their Catholic government. Champernowne took a hundred horsemen, one of these - away from home for the first time

- was the fifteen year old Ralegh.

A great deal now depended upon a successful alliance between England and the Protestant Princes. A day after Henry returned with Catherine from Cornwall to London he was summoned to Court to learn that on the recommendation of the Earl of Leicester he had been appointed Ambassador to the Protestant Princes of Germany.

The Queen's written instructions to Harry were detailed and appear to have been amplified by verbal directions. It is clear that he had a role as trade envoy as well as responsibility for negotiations over political and military partnership.

Alva had ended Spain's hands-off method of colonising the Netherlands: there was a new urgency for English overseas traders to reduce their reliance on Antwerp and diversify their lines of commerce. The German port of Hamburg had for some time been identified as the most desirable alternative trading centre: London meanwhile showed no signs of losing its almost complete dominance as the home centre.

Henry's role as trade envoy was to consolidate a recent commercial treaty between the London traders - organised by the Merchant Adventurers' Company - and their counterparts in Hamburg. His financial experience would play a part alongside his political and military expertise. He was required to prepare the way for a fleet of nearly thirty ships laden with wool and cloth, and gather intelligence about any Spanish plans for attacks on ships.

A further job, apparent from Henry's action but unspecified in his instructions, was to lay the foundations for a wider agreement with the German states, Denmark and Sweden, which would exclude Spain from the region.

He was instructed that, following the completion of this task, he must journey on to Heidelberg for negotiations with Frederick, Elector of the Palatinate, who was the German Prince most relevant to any possible Anglo-German alliance. In this endeavour Killigrew would be picking up on his first initiative in Heidelberg ten years earlier.

The twin operations were linked by an intention to divert the English government's first profits from the new trade into a loan for underpinning German military initiatives in France and the

Netherlands.

It is just possible that Harry was cynically set up by the Queen - or at least by Cecil and Leicester - who perhaps did not expect the military alliance to be forthcoming but wanted the French and Spanish to believe it might. There was a home audience who also needed to be convinced of the Queen's determination. Who better to send to talk to German Calvinists than a zealot of the new reformation who would not even have to act out his commitment? After all, was not the concept of friendship to kin and servants weaker than that of strategic urgency?

Henry set off from Harwich in bitter weather on 18th February 1569, accompanied by a German envoy, Dr Junius. This was one of the coldest winters of the century.

Shortly after midnight on his first day at sea, Harry's boat was battered by a ferocious northerly gale and almost cast up on the beaches of Holland. Having been preserved at Dieppe in the summer of 1562 Henry was now in further peril of a salty end among the cod and the skuas.

Suddenly the wind veered. Like Cromwell eighty years later Harry had little doubt about the governance of meteorology. 'God, I trust favouring the service whereunto I am appointed, did by a larger wind deliver us from hence', he wrote to Cecil later from a dry land-base. They struggled to the island of Heligoland, whose collusive links with the sea-dogs of the Fal have not been identified. Here the astonished inhabitants informed them that the Elbe was completely frozen.

Lame Hal and his companion then chartered a small craft and steered for the mainland. They were required to cut their way through ice in order to reach the opposite shore - a difficult and dangerous procedure. After resting briefly at the town of Ritzebuttel near the mouth of the Elbe, they crossed over the ice-clogged river and pushed on towards their destination.

At Hamburg they received a warm welcome. Cecil was informed by letter 'our merchants here do report that the lorde of this towne be glad of the coming of our ships and will be ready to pleasure our nation in that they may conveniently'.

Leaving on 12 March, the travellers still had four hundred miles to cover to reach Heidelburg. The countryside was swarming with German mercenary soldiers fighting on both sides in the war. Harry and the Doctor were twice nearly waylaid - by the Duke of Alva's cavalrymen and some disbanded troops of the Prince of Orange. Eventually Protestant princes provided them with escorts.

Henry had been instructed to assess Elector Frederick's proposals before indicating Elizabeth's conditions for making a loan. Her terms included evidence of an adequate measure of support for the war from other German princes, who had shown themselves reluctant to antagonise the Catholic powers, and valid sureties to cover the loan.

Whilst these preliminary discussions occurred Henry relaxed at the Court, and perhaps recovered weight lost on the journey. The Elector announced that he would need to consult the Prince of Saxony at Dresden, and asked Henry to return to Hamburg to reduce suspicions about his mission. The scenario of mutual caution between Queen and possible continental allies, which had unrolled at Havre, was being replayed, and as then, Harry must wait and pray. Each act of caution by one side reinforced the suspicions of the other in a downward spiral. Henry misjudged the Queen's likely response and sincerely talked up the English support.

On 24th May Harry was in Hamburg to watch the arrival of the English fleet, delayed by fear of Spanish attack. Philip too had hesitated before authorising such an openly aggressive act, and Alva, like John Killigrew in the Fal six months before, had to bite the bullet of frustration as prey passed out of his talons.

Henry Killigrew was frustrated as no English loan materialised. The Queen was unwilling to further the show-down with France and Spain, believing on this occasion that if provoked these two countries would settle their many differences. Yet the basic problem - Spanish troops just over the water - would remain for twenty years.

The Queen wrote to Killigrew, praising him for his diplomacy, but indicating her unwillingness to proceed. He stayed on in Germany, trying to persuade leaders to adopt a stance which would convince Elizabeth that they were reliable allies. They called a convention of Protestant states, whose conservatism and suspicion justified Elizabeth's caution. Protestants unwilling to take on the

Devil unless they were adequately provisioned.

In September 1569, seven months after his departure, Harry arrived back in London. Although he continued to bluff it out with foreign ambassadors, he must have known that the mission was a failure in the short term at least. However this second round of diplomacy, like the first in 1559, provided huffs of a wind which would blow stronger in years to come. This time round no secrecy was required: it served the Queen's purpose if France and Spain learnt that she was willing to negotiate with Germany.

This enterprise had also shown the Queen and Council that Killigrew, although he might be 'dull', as the Queen once described him, was still street-wise and sea-wise in spite of female company, a steady income and elevated connections. Had he not demonstrated that he could still juggle with allies needing encouragement and home governments possessing minimalist intentions? And might those links with Cornwall shortly be less of an embarrassment, quite an asset in fact? Would there be more work to do?

However, Henry might have too many competencies in his portfolio. As Smith comments, "clever men were suspect, men of courage esteemed to be turbulent, honest and just men accounted morose and not compliant enough, only the problem-solving servant thrived". Killigrew was all these things, as the Queen knew, and might be too good to be true.

QUICKER AND STOUTER

E ngland's foreign affairs stumbled through a short period of complexity during which Henry played leading roles in France then Scotland. His work in Scotland provides a particularly fascinating case-study of the intricacies of Tudor diplomacy and reveals his talents at their most developed.

The main aim remained to neutralise Spain's strength especially in the Netherlands. A new method emerged for achieving this: the Protestant influence in the English government surprised itself by strong support for an alliance with Catholic dominated France.

The maintenance of this alliance was central to English diplomacy, with Walsingham acting in the crucial role of resident Ambassador in France, mostly working in Blois. When he had to be recalled, for six months over 1571 - 2, Killigrew occupied the post, meeting Walsingham in Paris for exchange of briefs. Henry no doubt brought Francis up to date with the latest tortures and tortuousness of the still active Ridolphi affair.

Embassies at the time, by tacit agreement, were employed not only as homes for diplomats and diplomacy, but as centres of religious propaganda and military subversion. This embassy was no exception. Up front, Harry was engaged in persuading the French to reciprocate English advances, especially by withholding support of their kinswoman Mary, Queen of Scots, who was still the focus of plots against Elizabeth although detained in England.

Henry had become convinced that Mary must go. 'You must take her now for dead' he told the French government. His counter-espionage involved checking out French moves, such as support for

Mary by la Mothe, the French ambassador in London, who was politely informed that his behaviour was under investigation.

The French openly encouraged Mary's supporters for a little longer, and sent money. When this was intercepted they brazenly asked for it to be returned. Killigrew politely refused, suggesting that for the English to yield to this request might cause offence to many and damage the improved cross-Channel relationship. He also protested about a French private army which he had learnt was being formed.

As so often, Killigrew had to argue on two fronts. Not only in France but with his own Queen, who was extremely reluctant to take the final step against Mary. In February 1572 he wrote courageously and in vehement terms to Elizabeth, urging her to take action and invoking God on her side. He returned to England and, in an interview whose record has not survived, set about persuading her to marry the French king's younger brother, an ugly stunted teenager. However, he was as weary as everyone else (except the Queen herself) of these royal courtships. He emerged from this discussion to confide in la Mothe that he believed she would never marry - unless in fear of her life or her kingdom - and simply enjoyed being courted.

The world beyond diplomacy persisted. In 1571 Henry became the member for Truro in the new Parliament, which met for just two months. Two of his brothers were also there.

He continued his work as a Teller, delegating where necessary. A strong war was being waged inside the Exchequer: traditionalists were complaining about the unreliability of Tellers and trying to regain control over the receipt of royal revenue. In 1572 Cecil stepped in to support Mildmay, the Chancellor of the Exchequer, in issuing stringent new orders for Tellers. If this upset Killigrew, it was at this time that he was compensated by Cecil for all his troubles with the wardship of Jonathan Trelawny.

A new parliament sat in 1572, with Harry again member for Truro. It sat briefly in that year, and again early in 1576 and 1581. There is no record of a speech by Killigrew in any debate during his whole parliamentary career. Parliament did not play the complementary role in government which exists in the present time, but was beginning to assert itself, notably in seeking to protect the Queen's succession and arguing about religion. Henry's experience was recognised when he was chosen as one of a Committee of Both Houses which was set up to advise on dealing with Mary: following its work bills were drawn up seeking to put her on trial and to deprive her of the English succession.

During 1571 Cecil had been raised to the peerage as Lord Burghley. As he rose up, Norfolk and his friends went down, some condemned through confessions extracted under the rack and amplified by perjury at the trial. Burghley in his supremacy softened to no-one, cool with Killigrew and even Walsingham, friendless, remorseless.

Throckmorton had died, Francis Walsingham too rose up. Harry lost one ally but gained another. During the period from 1570 to 1572 Henry developed a close working and personal friendship with Walsingham. This man was almost Henry's double - their origins in the middle ranks of the gentry, religious radicalism, detached scepticism about their Queen, effective use of secrecy, willingness to engage in state terror. Walsingham differed in the extent of his single-mindedness and balance of judgement, his toughness under criticism from the Queen: he was the abler man and later succeeded Cecil as Principal Secretary. Conversely he less frequently shows the wry humour and endearingly vulnerable side which derived from Harry's apparent lack of political ambition.

They had almost certainly known each other as far back as the period when they were both in exile and spent time in Italy. Francis sported a neat Italianate beard; perhaps Henry wore one too, but no portrait of him has been identified from any stage in his life. Perhaps they had been acquainted even earlier during Edward's reign, when both as young men came under strong influence of radical protestant leaders. They had worked together in Cecil's circle in the 1650s and later in the Ridolphi affair.

Cecil and Walsingham, although not friends, worked together brilliantly. Their network of spies provided critical information in an age without a standing army or any organised system of law enforcement. Their political network, of which Bacon and Killigrew were important members, was the nearest anyone came to forming an elite, following the demise of the nobility. No merchant-based, military or religious elite rivalled them.

Elizabeth continued to resist the execution of Mary, but she was horrified and confused like everyone else when her newly cultivated French Catholic royal allies were implicated in the crowd massacres of Protestants in Paris on St Bartholomew's Day, August 1572. Here was sixteenth century paranoia and nastiness at its most appalling; nothing approaching death-dealing crowd frenzy ever occurred in Tudor England except under cover of battle in the field. However the Queen set reason above emotion and refused to break off the newly emerging understanding with France. She most reluctantly accepted the need for stronger action on the Scottish front, eventually even agreeing to the elimination of Mary.

Once more she turned to Henry to be at the front line of a vital endeavour. Could she set up someone else to murder Mary and keep her own hands clean? Harry would be the ideal agent to get the Protestant Scots to do the final deed.

Henry was already well briefed on Scotland, which was being riven by conflict between two factions. One was broadly Protestant and supported the young James as monarch, looking to England for alliance. Mary was backed by a rival faction of both religions which looked overseas to France and Spain. There was no obvious division on class lines, members of the nobility and gentry danced to pipes of either side.

Elizabeth - who perhaps wished that the weight of Scotland would fall into the North Sea as long as Killigrew could ensure that Cornwall would not then sink into the Channel - was predictably unwilling to support James' faction with open military aid, for fear of bringing French forces back to Scotland. However due in part to efforts of Killigrew and Walsingham in France, the French were now co-operating with England's plan to reconcile the two Scottish factions under James. Mary was now taken for dead.

Both factions were supposed to lead their troops out of Edinburgh. Are things ever so simple? James' supporters took over most of the town, with Mary's holed up high in the Castle on its formidable rock.

Henry, with his extraordinary ability for knowing the right people at the right time, could call on trusting relationships with key individuals on both sides. As Miller wrote: 'the fact that he was chosen to represent the English government in Scotland during a moment when the country seemed in great danger following the recent events in France (the Massacre of St Bartholemew), is an indication of the confidence which the Queen and her ministers placed in his ability'. To which one must add: their recognition of Henry's dark side. As Leicester put it later: 'Harry Killigrew is a quicker and stouter fellow than I took him for. He can deal roughly enough when it pleaseth him'. Here was a mission where Henry might need to draw on the Arwennack genius for helping people to be good neighbours, and to go credibly hawking in Liskeard when you have ordered the use of knives in Penryn.

Killigrew learnt that his official task was to underpin the local peace agreement, and bind it with mortar, but without compromising English independence of action. He was commanded to put the fear of God into both Scottish factions - fear especially that the French, although currently allies of the English in Scotland, were planning another careful massacre of Protestants (especially noble ones) - this time in the quiet corners of Edinburgh and Perth. As Scots knew, poisoning clan leaders or setting them at each other's thrones would be no difficult task. After this, he was to say, an army of French papists and rapists would descend to complete the subversion of the state.

He discovered that his unofficial job was more difficult than the crude act of persuasion within his official brief: he was to lay the groundwork for secretly delivering Mary for execution by her Scottish enemies.

To be informed of this extra-ordinary mission Hal was called to a private meeting with the Queen, Cecil and Leicester at Woodstock Palace near Oxford. His secret instructions have survived. He was to handle matters so that a proposal for Mary's delivery and execution would come from the Scots. The condition for turning Mary over was that her execution should occur immediately, before the French or anyone else could stop it. He must not under any circumstances divulge the English origins of this idea, the Queen added, and if this happened through his carelessness he would suffer dire punishment. Harry gave a solemn pledge to guard the secret as he would his life.

7th September 1572, he set off so urgently that he had no time to say goodbye to Catherine or his small children. Once again, the Great

North Road - Grantham, Tuxford, Wetherby. The ever shifting groundbase of horses and roads, the disharmonious descant of travelling servants and luggage bags.

Riding one hundred miles a day through the late summer, he pondered on a mission so vital and yet so apparently impossible. All attempts to push the Queen towards open support of the radical cause - in Germany, the Netherlands, Scotland and France - had so far failed. Was she really on board now? Did Harry wonder - perhaps not for the first time - whether some deeper pattern lay beneath his orders, a pattern as yet undiscerned by him, even a pattern whereby his friends were sending him out to fail?

Henry journeyed first to Tantallon where he called on Morton, the leader of James' party, whom he immediately identified as 'the only man for her Majesty to account for in this realm' - a judgment subsequently agreed by others. Then on to Stirling to meet Mar, acting as Regent to young King James' party. He also briefed a shadowy Scottish agent to raise with these men the matter of the transfer of Mary. As the Scots began to introduce conditions into any such deal - which inevitably called for some of the Queen's money - Harry realised that the idea could not be adequately discussed among the Scots without the loss of secrecy. To Burghley he wrote: 'these men be so devilled and uncertain in their doings as I cannot tell what to write of them, but of this your honour may be assured, I trust no one no farther than I see with my eyes or feel with my fingers'. Evil was a measurable force, paranoia a necessary political antenna.

Henry renewed his acquaintance with the dying but still fiery old Protestant leader John Knox. Soon the French reputation was being knifed in the streets by the scandalous news of the Paris massacre.

Leaving aside the secret matter, attempts to provide a lasting settlement between factions were held in irons by stubbornness of some leaders, especially supporters of Mary. Knox wrote to one of them, Maitland, who was bolted into Edinburgh Castle, that if he did not foresake his evil ways he would be 'dragged from his nest and hanged from a gallows with his face against the sun'.

Maitland it was who had played a strong part in getting Mary, Queen of Scots to argue for Harry's release after Rouen ten years earlier. Back in 1557 Killigrew had helped another of Mary's current supporters, James Melville, still his warm friend, to escape from the battle at St Quentin when they were on opposite sides during Henry's exile under the English Queen Mary. God predestines these ambiguities of service and obligation, man obeys.

Harry would not need telling that in a world of rapidly evolving alliances you could not serve in equal measure your religion, your Queen and your old friends.

As negotiations continued, Morton and Regent Mar offered terms for the execution of Mary which required Elizabeth to identify publicly with the handover. No speed, no secrecy. Henry unwisely sent off these obviously unacceptable terms to Burghley and Leicester, managing at the same time to give the impression that he had allowed the Queen's name to be brought into his discussions. As Miller comments, two blunders.

The granite reprimand from the Queen, transmitted by Burghley and Leicester, reduced Harry to a state of chronic anxiety and vomiting for several days. It was all a matter of his Cornish English, which had been misunderstood, he pleaded muddily, in a long and grovelling reply. He asked to be replaced by someone more capable.

As Miller observes, Harry 'lacked that total independence and fortitude which would have enabled him to disregard such pressures'. In this he differed from Cecil, Throckmorton and Walsingham, although they too knew the limits to which they could journey with the Monarch. However 'the natural buoyancy and firmness of his personality reasserted themselves'.

Henry's frightened reaction was normal in that fear-ridden age. Few who had served in the Court of Henry VIII or operated close to all-powerful Northumberland acting on behalf of Edward VI, and had seen the Crown assume all powers of aristocracy and church oligarchy including God's authority, would be happy to passively absorb acrid smoke from nostrils of an angry Tudor monarch.

Secret execution of Mary by Scots was soon dropped from the agenda. This aspect of the English initiative, based on a desire to capitalise and decapitalise on hysteria following the French massacre, had yielded very little, and Harry almost plummeted down with it. Perhaps a rare example of both Elizabeth and Burghley simultaneously losing their fine judgment: or were they testing the limits of what they could get away with - not too bothered about the consequences for Killigrew?

Concerning all other internal disagreements among Scots, Henry continued to use trusting relationships he enjoyed with both sides to prevent disintegration of dead-locked discussions and, where possible, to edge negotiations forward. He also employed subterfuge, strategic illness, well-timed withholding of English funds and vigorous persuasion.

He was notably successful in persuading Morton to accept the Regency after Mar died, with strong backing from the nobility of both factions. This development further isolated the extremists in the Castle, who were now looking to France to break the Anglo-French treaty by offering support.

It was now four months since Harry had arrived in Scotland. Christmas 1572 approached. Surrounded in the dour northern capital by squabbling factions, separated from his young family, what inner loneliness did he feel? His simplified religion provided no easy substitutes for the comfort given by magical protectors among saints and by chanting monks in candlelight fingering beads of forgiveness. A man prayed and waited for signs of his predestined fate.

Walsingham, who had returned to take over the diplomatic reins in France from Harry, was indicating that the French might seek to relieve the Marians in the Castle. Morton in Edinburgh was demanding English military support to breach the Castle and threatening to look elsewhere if it were not forthcoming.

Elizabeth as usual was refusing to commit forces or increase expenditure. Following Killigrew's secret visit to London in January 1573 she yielded, sending Henry off with more money followed by ordnance and military advisers on siege battery. On his return water was cut off from the Castle.

At this point in the Scottish matter Henry's strength as the outsider, the stranger, once more came in useful. Morton wanted to complete the isolation of the Castle by making concessions to Mary's other supporters, but without antagonising his own militants. He therefore asked Killigrew to move him on these in the presence of the Scottish Lords. In February many of the former supporters of the Scottish Queen attended Killigrew's lodging at Perth to agree to a pacification.

'All was done in my house to her Majesty's great honour and credit... Now there remains but the Castle'.

Several weeks passed in preparations for siege-war. Henry's spies reported further plotting between Maitland and the French. The Castle leaders were playing for time, resisting final peace bids in the hope of French military support, which was never forthcoming. Henry made arrangements for transport of men and supplies, and for exchange of hostages. He argued vigorously against Elizabeth's predictable prevarications before she finally committed her men to the siege.

500 English arquebusiers and 140 pikemen entered Edinburgh on 25th April. Harry had advised his government that the sight of troops and guns would force the Castle to give in without a fight. This was a reasonable prediction, but the psychology of Castle leaders could not permit surrender. When under pressure primitive distinctions between Good and Evil re-asserted themselves. It is better to be dead than...

Henry now found himself keeping the peace between English and Scottish allies: the Scots were accused of planning to seize English guns and grab Castle treasure for themselves. Informants assured him that these were false rumours: he wrote to Burghley 'it might be answered that the sky may fall and we shall catch larks'.

Aware no doubt that Elizabeth would be counting the cost of every day of the siege (which he had advised would not be necessary), the English slowness in laying batteries exasperated him. As a son of the Governor of Pendennis, still lame from Rouen, Harry could not be expected to stand aside from the final assault on the Castle. As an old soldier he did not think very highly of some of the English officers, fresh and pink from their soft lives at Court and perhaps unduly impressed by the height of the bastion.

To speed up work on batteries Harry spent two successive nights with pick and spade helping to dig gun mounts within range of enemy artillery. Diggers were often buried by earth displaced by enemy cannon shot, which showered over the mounts.

Ten days of hard pounding were required for the siege to have effect. On 26th May Killigrew attended a parley of the interested parties: next day the Castle capitulated.

Castle leaders were now in English hands. When Morton demanded execution their peril was great, although some had once enjoyed good relations with England, including with Burghley. They pleaded for their lives.

Henry meanwhile scoured the Castle, uncovering evidence that Maitland had appealed for help from Spain as well as from those Catholic French who had sparked off the Paris massacre. He wrote to London vigorously opposing leniency to these leaders, but knowing the Queen favoured James Melville he asked her to save James' brother from execution. Elizabeth shared Henry's view on these matters and also his attention to detail: she ordered the English commander to hand Maitland and his confederates to Morton for execution, but persuaded Morton to spare Melville. 'An English gentleman, my old friend Harry Killigrew' James Melville later described him.

At the end of June 1573 Harry was at last recalled to England after ten months of intensive service.

This period in Scotland was probably Henry's greatest achievement. He was an outsider to the main conflict, which could have disintegrated into civil war, chaos and bloodshed, thus upsetting the tentative accord with France. He used to the full his status as an interested stranger, bringing to bear his patience and evident trust-worthiness, combined with an underlying ruthlessness, in order to tease the Scots towards a solution which they could not have found for themselves.

If it was normal for an ambassador to vomit when the Queen was cross, Hal was abnormal in his apparent lack of serious enemies (if these had existed they would be identifiable today among the considerable detail of his life). He was also exceptional by virtue of his acceptance in trust by rival factions both at home and abroad, and also by his capacity to embody for a lifetime an extreme and potentially paranoid religious mission in a highly anxiety-ridden age yet without developing a sickly personality.

His achievement was widely recognised. Morton wrote to Burghley praising his 'experience and dexterity in doing, as well for the universal good liking conceived of him and his good behaviour, both by this nobility and the whole people'. He would always be welcome back.

On his journey home Harry may have reflected on the phenomenon of the diplomat, the curious role of the stranger, and wondered if the Cornish possessed a particular aptitude in this role.

The diplomat, unlike other kinds of traveller, does not come today and go tomorrow: it is more subtle than that. Rather he is the wanderer with no plans to move on. He comes today and stays tomorrow, but remains the potential wanderer who has not overcome the freedom of coming and going.

This kind of stranger (as the sociologist Simmel pointed out) is an important member of the community - the confessor or counsellor - an outsider who is used by the community as a vault for confidences, a traveller in secret fears and ambitions.

The Cornish were experienced strangers. Saxons understood something of this when they called Cornwall 'the land of the strangers': by their definition of the word, not a distant foreigner, not the Icelandic fisherman or Barbary sailor, but someone just over the edge of the everyday familiar world.

The Cornish man or woman is born on this edge and will always be a member of the larger kingdom but also not a member. If he is required to travel outside his county he may have a unique opportunity to become the neutral adviser, not implicated in the settled community, squatting roundly in his own integrity. When Queen Elizabeth stated that the Cornish gentry were 'all born courtiers with a becoming confidence' she confirmed their status by her very choice of words with their resonant ambiguity. Henry and his brother William, both close to the Queen, were specialists in absorbing the confidences of others - those trusting gifts of secret information - in order themselves to become confident.

Henry, who had learnt to be a useful outsider in London, had then found that his skills were needed on a wider canvas. Having used the stranger in their homeland, the English community orders him on to far-off places where English interests depend on uniting factions, or bringing other countries to a common accord. Full of temporary invested power, the outsider's success depends on whether he is received in each new venue as a necessary stranger.

Did anyone question the loneliness of the job, the continuous assaults on your sense of who you are, the stresses? Henry fell back on ideology and on the versatile Killigrew family whom he seemed still to carry packed tightly into his soul, remembering the two-headed eagle glaring superbly in two directions from the castle battlements.

Harry was beginning to see the results of his work. During the last ten years since Rouen he had persistently tried to quicken the pace of Protestant challenges to European Catholicism, sometimes overtaking conservative Elizabeth's policies to find himself over-exposed.

The Scottish trip was much more successful in everyone's terms. He had persuaded the Queen to come up front, and outmanoeuvred the French. In the course of this personal success he had overcome a serious set-back caused by a major error.

Harry was restored to Catherine and the small daughters in time to enjoy the English summer. What would be in store next for the forty-five year old man? Would the Queen reward him well, enabling him to live the more leisurely gentleman's life which he desired, or play on his idealism to project him into another nearly impossible mission? If he had to go into action again, would his advancing age lead to caution and loss of energy when fire was ordered, or would his courage stand up?

HARVEST IN THE BARN

Henry must have received an extended welcome when he returned in July 1573 to his house in St Paul's Churchyard.

Around this time Catherine was in poor health, which perhaps had been long-standing. She also sought help for her religious questionings.

While he was away in Scotland his brother William, whose own house was close to Henry's by St Pauls, provided solid support to the young family. In that year William had been elevated from a minor court office to the more significant one of Groom of the Chamber. Burghley's intercession had helped in obtaining this post.

Since their marriage Catherine and Henry had probably discovered congenial company among each others' friends. From Cornwall those who demonstrated the rounded life included Francis Godolphin, Jonathan Trelawny senior (who had just died, his son left in Henry's hands), young Richard Carew: did these weave a sympathetic lyric for the reflective and bookish Catherine?

In that year Catherine's sister Elizabeth, Hoby's widow, married again, to John Russell, second son of Francis, Earl of Bedford: definitely the kind of marriage Burghley would approve of. The Earl was a senior Privy Councillor, a strong but not fundamentalist protestant and the most powerful influence across the whole of the West Country: two of his daughters had married respectively the Earl of Cumberland and Ambrose Dudley, Earl of Warwick - Robert's brother. Russells and Dudleys now, as well as Cecils, are brothers and sisters to the Killigrews.

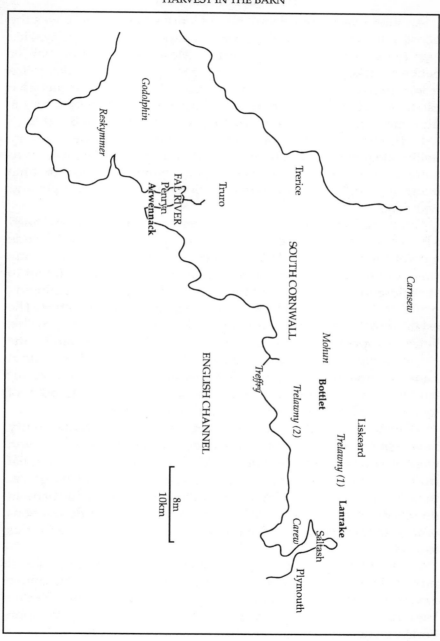

Another reason for celebration at Henry's homecoming was the boost to the family's standing from acquiring a new property. This was the Cornish manor of Lanrake, close to the Devon border between Liskeard and Saltash, lying among the low hills five miles from the coast at the head of a quiet estuary. This potentially lucrative estate was given by the Queen to Henry in May as a reward for his diplomatic services, again following the intervention of Burghley.

In the years immediately after the Edinburgh siege Harry deliberately moved back to rural life, dividing himself between two landscapes - Cornwall and the London countryside. For the time being at least, he had adequately explored the role of stranger and wanderer.

Unlike his brother William, Henry does not seem to have possessed a house in Cornwall (the estate of Lanrake apparently did not include a decent residence) nor to have taken steps to acquire one. In any case Lanrake was not the place to establish a dynasty, you had to stay close to Court to clip off the first shoots of poisonous clinging plants of slander or treachery as they swayed in your direction. The estate may have seemed unacceptably close to a site for possible lightning Spanish raids: in 1574 the Spanish planned a raid on the Fal, estuaries eastwards would have suited just as well. The estate at Lanrake remained with the family after Harry's death, and on this land his son built Ince Castle which now weaves a counterpoint of rosy mellow brick and grey slate against tidal waters.

As well as his house in London and the estate at Lanrake Henry now also enjoyed a property at Hendon, seven miles to the north west of London. Here he often resided with his family as a relief from London's in-fighting, noise, heat and disease, watching over the planting and harvesting of his family and lands - a husband in no way different from William Carnsew, whose colourful descriptions of this rhythm on his Cornish estates have happily survived for us to read.

The location and ownership of the Hendon estate presents a small puzzle. Detailed contemporary records do not show Henry's name among Hendon landowners. The suggestion that Killigrew rented Hendon Place from Sir Edward Herbert and later from Sir John Fortescue (a close associate of Burghley) is a possibility.

My own suggestion derives from studying the local records: these indicate that in 1574 'a Mrs Reskymmer holdeth a messuage' at Burrows, which is surely a clue. Mrs Reskymmer (her surname before her marriage) was the grandmother of Henry's new ward Jonathan Trelawny, and a rich heiress in her own right. The Reskymmers were close neighbours of Arwennack, enjoying their estates near Helston. It seems too much of a coincidence that this lady was owning property in Hendon so far from Cornwall, and close to Henry and Catherine, unless as part of financial arrangements of wardship. The Hendon property may have been a home for both her fatherless grandson and his keeper. Jonathan would need to be close to London to benefit from Killigrew's contacts - soon he entered Cecil's private forcing school for brilliant youngsters.

Jonathan's widowed mother Anne remarried, to Henry's Cornish neighbour Sir William Mohun, so she is unlikely to have played much part in the London upbringing of Jonathan.

In later years Killigrew's family became even more closely related to both Trelawnys and Mohuns. One of his daughters married Jonathan and another married Reginald Mohun, a son from Anne's remarriage - so two of Anne's children married two of Henry's.

Relations between Killigrews and Mohuns had not always been good. Ann's new father-in- law was the Mohun who, in 1565, dared to haul Harry's father before the Privy Council with a string of charges. Few dared to deal with old Sir John in that manner.

In 1574, before he could have become fully acquainted with Lanrake Killigrew launched out again, buying from the Earl of Huntingdon a large estate at Bottlet on the opposite (west) side of Liskeard. This estate, one of the largest that this rich but financially troubled radical protestant earl ever put on the market, cost Harry the considerable sum of three and a half thousand pounds: this sum can be compared to the total Parliamentary grant of £26,000 made annually to the Queen in the relative peace of the late seventies.

Henry's purchase was not a speculative investment using borrowed money with a view to a quick sale, nor was it purchased on behalf of his ward. All or some of Bottlet remained in his possession to be bequeathed in his will.

Harry continued to work as a Teller, and no doubt on more secret business. He wrote to Francis Walsingham in 1574 'I had thought to see you before now, but my harvest is not all in the barn which causes my absence for a while longer unless you advise me to the contrary'. This message seems an example of the elaborate code employed by Cecil, Walsingham and others in their communications on state and personal security, and probably refers to some complex counter-espionage. It is unlikely that Killigrew was needed to supervise the storage of winter fodder or the making of quince preserve.

It remains just possible however that through this communication Harry may have been quietly advising his friend to lead a less single-minded life. Francis was often ill in the Queen's service, and in spite of his extraordinary talent and success Elizabeth failed to reward him at that or any later time. Henry may have been telling Francis that he did not envy his friend his greater worldly success.

Burghley too, since he handed on the Principal Secretaryship, had spent a few years trying to broaden the scope of his activities but continuously succumbed to forces which pulled him back to the obsessive political life. Smith wrote of the period that 'as there is no acceptable alternative to political success - loyal opposition, achievement in some other occupation, or relief in direct action - mental anguish and neurotic behaviour are to be expected'.

1574 witnessed further attempts by Henry's Cornish associates to develop profitable enterprises in the New World. Formidable Richard Grenville in particular was planning an expedition, but the Queen needed him at home so it was led by another. Whether Henry gave financial support is not clear, but as the backdrop to an enterprise ten years later Grenville appointed Henry Killigrew and Francis Godolphin as trustees of his estate.

Killigrew was now in the greatest danger of his life, not from political disgrace or the assassin's cup, not from idealism, but from his own career success. Talent leads to offers of more responsibilities - ambition and sense of duty tempt you to put aside what is most enjoyed. The impact of such sacrifice can be lethal to soul and body.

He was increasingly convinced that diplomatic service was a career of strictly limited appeal. Not only rupturing family relations, exposing the diplomat to instant career-death for the most momentary lapse of judgement, and placing you in permanent physical danger from cannon-fire or storms: it also hit the pocket, certainly in comparison with other offices. Henry was not alone in this attitude, Walsingham had been extremely unwilling to accept his promotion to France and a number of his potential successors had been reluctant too. The last straw was probably the moral tone of some of the back-room work. Walsingham (ruthless, unimpressionable) wrote in 1578: 'I will hereafter take my leave of foreign services... seeing men are so ready to pick quarrels and to deprave careful, painful and good meaning'.

The nation needed these men's skills. Elizabeth was ambitious in her foreign policy, not merely to prevent setbacks but to advance her prestige and influence. To an extraordinary degree she achieved this not by war but by peaceful means. By the early 1570s she had shown Europe her brilliant Machiavellian politics as she broke or shifted alliances with astonishing rapidity, using ambiguity and deceit to maximum effect, concealing actions of doubtful legality under spurious justifications. Her policy depended to the utmost on watchfulness, good intelligence and day and night diplomatic skill.

Elizabeth, with Burghley as main instrument, wielded most of the power over a life-time, but neither ever travelled overseas, neither had military experience: their judgment lacked a dimension on this account, which others had to fill. Leicester and Essex were disasters in foreign parts, Smith kept losing his temper, Hatton and Huntingdon never ventured abroad.

Harry was one of a small cadre of excellent diplomats on whom Government relied, often far more than these men wished. Because of the nature of the Queen's chosen method of prosecuting foreign policy they were in effect the warriors of the nation. Although in popular memory it is Drake, Grenville, Ralegh, Hawkins who are remembered as the leading edge of the English advance overseas - all of them west countrymen - the shadowy figures of Throckmorton, Killigrew, Walsingham, Randolph and a handful of others were for three and a half decades the real overseas force to be reckoned with. Of these Killigrew is the only one who also fought with gun and sword, the only west countryman.

Henry and Catherine were thrown onto the defensive at this time. The slow and unobtrusive advance of radical Protestantism was being halted during these years, both abroad and at home. In 1573 England was able to settle its differences with both France and Spain (the Spanish were bothered by the Turks again), and Elizabeth abandoned the Dutch Protestants. This reversal dismayed English militants who saw the Netherlands as a crucible of religious evolution.

At home Elizabeth planted both regal feet to stubbornly obscure the map of religious change. Her religious policy was the one aspect of her governance where she became increasingly out of tune with her people, at all levels of society. Abandoning her normal genius for holding the consensus, she fell back on primitive paranoia and splitting between black and white. She failed to see that during most of her reign radical Protestantism was moderate in its aims. Reformers, led now by a generation younger than Latimer and Cooke, shared the same world view as more traditional Protestants and agreed too on most of the theology.

Radicals were seeking to influence the national church, not split from it. There was little fanaticism about worship, nor abhorrance of a good time in bed-chamber, theatre and table, nor persecution of others: little therefore of the aspects of 'puritanism' which became familiar in the seventeenth century - it is not an accurate term to apply to Elizabeth's reign.

Church organisation was the dog-pit of argument, and the Queen's main bones of contention were the development of freelance preaching and the pattern of informal and semi-formal meetings among clergy and others. Even leading traditionalists favoured some of these developments, and in 1576 the Archbishop of Canterbury refused the Queen's order to suppress the meetings and was himself suspended from office for six years until his death. Unfortunate Grindal, no Becket he.

The main impetus for the innovatory meetings was a sincere pastoral concern to improve the support given to clergy, including aiding their understanding of the Bible, so they could provide a little more pastoral care to the spiritually hungry population.

Elizabeth knew that the reformers were under the influence of Swiss Calvinist presbyterianism - with its more radical concern to formalise the participation of the laity in church affairs. Although for the most part this participation was intended to be under the continuing leadership of the ordained ministry, there were clear calls to curtail the extensive power of bishops and end the close links between church and state. Here was the rub for Elizabeth and the traditionalists. The paranoid principle took over - as James I came to spout: 'No Bishop No King'. One Terrible Thing will always lead to Another.

Some of these religious experiments may seem dour and intrusive in our age, but were a logical extension of religious orthodoxy at the time. Above all it was orderly. In 1570 the town of Northampton experimented with presbyterian church government - at the invitation of the local gentry under the protection of the Earl of Leicester. The experiment produced the most complete example of a Genevan Calvinist set-up which England ever suffered. Clergy and magistrates jointly enforced morality, citizens were compelled to go to church, listen to sermons and have Bible lessons. Ministers met regularly for mutual criticism. Northampton has not recovered to this day. Inevitably divisions existed among the radicals which provided an opening for opponents of the venture. Dudley attempted to protect this innovation against hostility from the local bishop, in spite of knowing that the Queen disapproved. After a couple of years it had to be rolled back.

Disorderly extremism only grew towards the end of the reign, under pressure from the Queen's successful division and suppression of radical Protestantism. There will always be a few fanatics, especially in an age without psychotropic medication, but it was twenty years before the Bible was being given the very force of magic which the reformation had been seeking to remove. Only then did the Elizabethans suffer the slug-plagues of kill-joys satirised in Nashe, Jonson and Shakespeare. Only then did believers seek to set up separate sects and other arrangements under obsessive and contorted systems of lay leadership, experiments which would take a further half century to produce more mature forms such as Quakerism.

The Killigrews' support of radical figures becomes obvious at this time. In 1570 the reformer Dering had harangued the Queen to her face on her responsibility to the Church, followed by similar expositions of the failings of Cecil and the Archbishop. This did not prevent Catherine from carrying out a detailed and lengthy correspondence with Dering. Cartwright, who in 1570 had been expelled from his professorial chair and in 1572 from his fellowship was also undoubtedly part of their circle at this time: he later benefited from Henry's patronage. In 1574 one radical leader, Travers, who in 1578 Henry strongly supported, published the first major exposition of radical church government. Henry's own attitude to protestant reform has not survived in written form and can only be inferred. He actively sought the appointment of radical priests, as with William Ramsay as far back as 1559. He was closely involved in the so-called London conference (a form of on-going Presbyterian church organisation), and actively promoted its extension.

That Harry was not willing to countenance the more extreme manifestations of change is evident from his membership, in 1581, of a Parliamentary Committee against the Family of Love. His dislike of these 'anabaptist extremes' may not however have caused him to rejoice when in 1575 some anabaptists were burnt to death close to his front door. What was anabaptism anyhow?: the puritan-hating historian Rowse described it as a 'distinguished undoctrinal freemasonry'.

In the early seventies Harry could afford to take a few risks in standing against the Queen in his support for religious change. Dudley's courageous leadership of the radical movement was decisive (Leicester was no puritan, he also formed his famous troupe of players). Other powerful supporters included Huntingdon, Lord Chancellor Bacon (Harry's brother in law) - who after the Accession had played a key role in appointing reform-minded if not radical bishops - and Walsingham. Burghley too, partly from conviction but also at the instigation of Mildred, was sympathetic if usually a little detached.

The general population provided a sympathetic if not fanatical backdrop to the reformers and their political protectors. Godliness was respected as well as respectable, and the highest prestige was enjoyed by righteously living families, especially top families. As one historian wrote about Huntingdon, he won renown not for his innovations and patronage in education but because he placed his adherence to the reformed religion before everything else.

The major battles over religious change were a few years off. Meanwhile the Killigrews could hope to enjoy some respite from Harry's travels. Their household must have resembled Lady Margaret Hoby's, with its daily round of family prayers (morning and evening), personal meditation and examination of conscience, frequent attendance at sermons, and the sacraments on weekdays and Sundays.

Households such as these were as important for spreading the influence of reformed and informed Protestantism as the part played by recusant establishments of greater fame for spreading Catholicism.

It must have come as a huge swipe in the face when, in the summer of 1574, only a year since his return from Scotland, the Queen asked Killigrew to go back. An ambassador was needed to consolidate the settlement there. The work included sorting out disputes between officials at the Anglo-Scottish frontier.

While in Scotland he also cross-examined English pirates who were harrying Scottish merchant shipping, and may have surprised the pirates with his close knowledge of the tricks of that trade. He observed the precocity of the eight year old King James, perhaps nurturing seedlings of favour whose flowering permitted William Killigrew to stay a senior court official for twenty years after James' accession to the English throne.

This short summer embassy in Scotland passed off uneventfully, but it may have seemed quite long enough to Catherine. She may additionally have feared that Henry would be recalled from Scotland only to be sent over to France or the Netherlands. It was perhaps this occasion when Catherine asked her sister to intercede with Burghley to relieve Henry of this mission. The poem in Latin which she sent to Mildred has survived in indifferent translation:

If, Mildred! by thy care he be sent back, who I request,
    A sister good thou are to me, yea better, yea the best:
But if with stays thou keep'st him still, or send'st where seas may part
    Then unto me a sister ill, yea worse, yea none thou art;
If go to Cornwall he shall please, I peace to thee foretell;
    But, Cecil! if he set to seas, - I war denounce. - farewell.

Scottish Regent Morton wrote to Burghley and Leicester in appreciation of these ambassadorial services but Harry may well have hoped that he had seen the last of Edinburgh in summer or winter.

1575 was in most respects a good year for England. Peace with France and Spain seemed assured while the Spanish were busy with Turks. Whereas Philip was bankrupt, in England debt was nearly reduced and trade was good. The channel ports, which only five years previously had been fortifying themselves against Spain, now welcomed their fleet on a courtesy visit.

In July Leicester organised the greatest of all the spectacles for the Queen which he laid on in his castle home at Kenilworth. The youthful Shakespeare may have attended this event just down the road from Stratford, and stored the details in his memory. In May Henry had provided his patron with ideas for fireworks and pageants which he had acquired from an Italian acquaintance (but probably not Ridolphi): among proposals was a scheme to fire live cats and dogs into the air. No doubt Killigrew and his family made plans to attend.

It was not to be. That summer would be spoilt too, and Catherine would prepare the young Killigrew daughters - there were now two or three of them and more to come - to see their father off on the road again. In June 1575 Henry had to toil back up north. This man of nearly fifty years, carrying heavy responsibilities as an Exchequer official, whose wife in that year continued to be unwell, cannot have welcomed the demand.

On this visit a serious disagreement broke out between Morton and Queen Elizabeth concerning an affray which occurred on the border about the time Henry reached Scotland. News reached the Queen at Kenilworth when she was enjoying the entertainments which Harry was missing. Incensed at what she judged to be Scottish aggression, her reaction promised to be out of all proportion and to threaten the roots of new accord between the two lands - which Harry had been sent north to promote.

Killigrew worked with Huntingdon, Lord President of the North in this affair (Huntingdon had sold him Bottlet the previous year). They were used as the messenger for the Queen's outrage. Henry received another of her sharp reprimands for his own behaviour during the immediate aftermath of this affray, which again she judged as too conciliatory: 'we must charge you with your dark and slight kind of advertisement whereby you show yourself not so careful of our service... You receive such demands at their hands that so much touch us in honour without making any reply to the same...'

Henry wrote despairingly to Leicester, asking to be recalled if renewed hostility were to break out. However, in spite of risking accusations of toning down the Queen's tantrum, he and the Earl of Huntingdon considerably diluted the venom of her communications.

Elizabeth refused to follow up early diplomatic success by adequately supporting the new Protestant anti-French group now ascendant in Scotland. For less than two thousand pounds in sweeteners paid to Morton and a few Protestant nobles, Killigrew said, she could have held the line. Even before he left Scotland for home he witnessed the beginning of internal unrest which eventually led to the downfall of Morton, further internal strife and pro-French behaviour damaging to England.

Personal worries assailed Harry on this Scottish trip. Catherine was spending the summer at the Hendon estate, but the plague had spread there and killed one of his servants, leaving his wife so ill he feared for her life. He also suffered a disorder in his legs, which was not soothed when on the return journey his thoughtless horse trod on his foot, depriving him of the nail of his big toe. The State Papers have preserved his letter to Walsingham: the pain was so great he could not put a boot on his foot. We are not told whether this was the foot in which he was already lame, but he cannot have looked a happy figure as he was helped off his horse at Hendon to be reunited with his family.

Henry presumably attended the session of the 1572 parliament which sat during February and March of 1576. As spring approached, he must have hoped and definitely prayed for no further outings to Scotland. How wistfully must his thoughts have turned to his Cornish cousins settling into a new season. William Carnsew, whose diary covers this year, spent April worrying about his lambs, organised the mending of a well and the making of stakes, sold tree-bark to a tanner, and wondered about the conquests of the Turks in

Europe. Tempestuous John Killigrew called at Carnsew's house on the 8th and borrowed a horse - 'for that his was tired' - to help him on his way to the Assizes at Launceston. That would have been John's manner - pressuring his fellow gentry, a difficult man to refuse. He came back four days later, presumably with the horse.

Carnsew notes that John had been awarded a knighthood in March, whose ceremony occurred at the end of the year. As one historian noted, a remarkably cynical appointment even by the standards of the day, and not easy to interpret. Surely not the hand of Burghley here, unless he was trying to pave the way for Henry to be knighted - it would be hard to elevate the younger before the elder son. The diary also notes that John was involved in a 'great fray' with another gentleman in Truro in October. John was always at war with anyone who stood in his way.

In 1576 the English peace accords with France and Spain held up, and some Dutch Protestants, resenting betrayal and possessing a good navy, began to vent their anger against English shipping. In return the English government sought to retaliate, and it is interesting that the Dutch ships seized were those vessels lying in the Fal roads. Lines of communication covering three hundred miles were remarkably good.

Whatever Henry may have thought about his brother's knighthood - it would be another fifteen years before his own remarkable service was recorded in the same way - he cannot have been pleased about the Dutch ships. The radical protestant faction in England wanted to help the Netherlands become independent from Spain and consolidate the reformed religion. Elizabeth wished colonial rule by Spain to continue, as long as it was imposed from a more tactful distance. The Dutch - who on many matters had been self-destructively divided - achieved an exemplary degree of internal accord in that year, and might have expected a political pay off: this was never forthcoming.

1576 probably saw a period of tension between the Queen and Henry. Presumably he was still an unfeed Gentleman of the Chamber, so remained close to Elizabeth, but he can only have been dismayed when, to complement her foreign policy which disregarded the claims of radical Protantism abroad, she set about the suppression of reforms within the church at home, especially the local meetings and conferences, which finally led a year later to the downfall of the Archbishop.

Elizabeth must have observed that Henry stuck to his culverins over politics and religion, never crawled to her on any matter, nor betrayed his confederates. She must have respected him, even when he pleaded to be taken from the front-line if his position became ambiguous.

The Queen was hard to influence over religion but she could not control the appointment of every new parson. The gentry would usually decide. Carnsew was continuously lobbied for the whole year concerning the benefice of St Minver near Wadebridge, and he supported Giles Creed, a Fellow of Exeter College, Oxford for this post. It was an important matter for William, coming up again and again in his diary. Money changed hands and Giles even entered his dreams. In November he agreed to support an approach to Henry Killigrew (no Harry or Hal here) who would wield influence with those making the final decision.

Three times that year Catherine and Harry comforted themselves with visits to Burghley's great establishment at Hatfield. Relations with many of the key figures - Leicester, Walsingham, Burghley - remained good.

Catherine's father, Sir Anthony Cooke, died in 1576. He had apparently been back-sliding: there was no record of recent involvement in any religious campaigning, in fact he appointed a slack minister to the church of which he held the advowson, and left no charitable bequests in his conventionally written will.

In December the gentry in the country houses heard about Archbishop Grindal's defiance of the Queen, perpetrated in the second week of the month. The roads between London and Cornwall were busy. Creed, who had set off from Cornwall on 26th November on his vital journey to London, may have learnt about Grindal's courageous act when he arrived. Perhaps he saw Henry at this time. On 19th December Carnsew dreamed again of Giles, that he came home without the benefice but 'was promised to have it shortly'. The following day the real Creed completed the round trip - twenty four days - holding his letters patent for St Minver.

Perhaps on his homeward journey Giles Creed passed the eastward progress of John Killigrew and his retinue. John received his knighthood on Christmas Day. Did Henry and Catherine celebrate the end of their year by providing hospitality for this incongruous company?

It had been a mixed eighteen months. Reprimands from Elizabeth, Catherine's illness, Henry's injury, setbacks to Presbyterians at home and in the Netherlands. Tudor monarchs had to be watched, yet the tension with the Queen might turn out to be an undisguised blessing if it meant no more days on the road to Edinburgh.

The Killigrew's personal difficulties, their political and religious disagreements with the government, these threw them onto the defensive, and must have led Catherine and Henry towards the reassessment which occurs when life is in the middle of its way.

LADY MARY
BURIES CHAIRS.

A part from a brief spying holiday in 1578, Henry stayed in England from 1576 to 1585. He never served purely as a diplomat again, but would have other overseas tasks to perform: England had moved on and its most experienced overseas operators would be needed not only for negotiations but also as proto-type colonial governors or minders of the Queen's adolescent generals.

Henry's time was channelled into his occupations as a Teller and Gentleman of the Privy Chamber, with an additional stream of minor duties. Much of his work may have been informal, subversive and unrecorded: in later years there are more glimpses of this from documentation.

In 1576 the Spanish Armada, Great Invasion Attempt, Philip's personal disaster, was still over a decade in the future, and during this period Elizabeth continued to twist and turn in order to avoid war, with the same limited objectives in relation to King Philip's troops in the Low Countries.

Elizabeth was mortified when the Dutch refused to do things according to her agenda. 1577 was a critical year in Dutch attempts to throw off Spanish colonial rule completely and govern themselves (Turks were troubling Philip again). However, many in the Netherlands did not want too much aggravation, they valued their trade with Spain and preferred to keep relationships as sweet as possible.

Towards the end of the year she seriously contemplated sending a large force and finance to aid the Dutch leader William the Silent in his efforts to oust the Spanish army. This force would have been commanded by Leicester.

A close friend who shared Henry's religious views found himself sent as Ambassador to William the Silent. Davison had been Harry's secretary in Scotland ten years earlier. Although the younger man and also a Calvinist, he later advanced beyond Henry to be Principal Secretary. At this time Harry no doubt experienced his usual ambivalence: desire to serve the cause but relief to be at home. He limited his action to writing encouragingly to Davison 'if my Lord of Leicester come over you shall see me there, God willing'.

The plan for a English military expedition was abandoned. Meanwhile without openly challenging Spain, the English engaged in spoiling tactics. The Queen had no difficulty in coaxing West Country sea-farers to play their part: she was able to persuade the enraged Spanish that forays on their shipping were nothing to do with her and stern action was being taken. Stern action consisted of setting up a Cornish Commission of Piracy to seek out and punish offending pirates, headed by law-abiding hidalgo landsman, newly knighted Sir John Killigrew.

The Receiver of piracy fines for England was Henry Killigrew. Was this another cynical appointment? That seems unlikely, given Harry's rectitude: more probably an administrative convenience, one of the four Tellers would presumably have to be named. This role might actually protect him from his Arwennack relations and provide a clear excuse to stand aside from them.

The Spanish may have wondered when Sir John would convene this Commission. When it finally tumbled to work headed by someone else, it could not conceal that many of the leading gentry had been involved in fencing stolen goods. Peter Killigrew lent the pirates the key to his cellar, at the cost of five hundred fish. He supplied them with cattle, absorbing in return two tons of iron horseshoes, some hogsheads of wine and thirty or forty sacks of rye, which he sold on. A number of gentlemen were later fined for their part in these transactions, the money finding its way eventually no doubt to the Receiver.

Following her routine, in 1577 Elizabeth visited the Bacons at Gorhambury, near St Albans. Beneath the calm a chilly war against

Spain was being wound up like a siege instrument, with provocative suppression of Catholics at home and harrassment of Spanish interests around the world.

The rhetoric too intensified. The country felt increasingly on the brink of the unknown, possibly of disaster. The demonic presence of the Enemy was felt in every dark corner, a potential traitor sidled up to every conversation. Defeat would be God's as well as England's.

Cruelty had always been easy to justify if the state was at risk. As hostility increased people found more reasons for necessary barbarisms.

Henry was in Cornwall during the summer of 1577 when Sheriff Richard Grenville broke onto the offensive against Catholics. On 30 November 1577 a leading Catholic, Cuthbert Mayne, was barbarously executed at Launceston, the first Catholic martyr of the reign anywhere in England. Grenville - even his knighthood came after John Killigrew's - orchestrated the arrest and trial, including packing the grand jury with Sir John and other anti-Catholics. Henry Killigrew wrote to Davison approvingly: 'an archpriest has been hanged and quartered'. In his letter he enclosed a copy of a confession by another Catholic apprehended in London.

It seems likely that Henry was carrying out interrogations at this time for Walsingham, although surviving evidence relates to later years. An age no different from ours in giving itself the brutal benefit of the doubt against suspected terrorists in wartime, but with greater certainty that God's will was being done, more intense paranoia during daylight and night-time.

Also in November Drake set off on his voyage which eventually became the second circumnavigation of the globe, over fifty years since Magellan first achieved this. He started badly: on 16th November the five ships were forced by a storm into the Fal estuary where they stayed a week before returning to Plymouth for a refit. Sir John was perhaps at the Assizes, not available to launch pinnaces at midnight for relieving ships of stores: but for this distraction, would Drake have got to sail around the world?

Drake's voyage had been a close secret, even Burghley apparently did not know, at least until the plans were leaked to him. The intention was probably to harrass Spanish interests on the Pacific coast of America, with no intention of circumnavigation. Henry wrote to Davison; '...if he do not miscarry, his journey will yield much light to our navigation. I make no small acount of that man'.

Henry's home-spun routines continued. Plague infested Hendon in December 1577. Drake reached north Africa fourteen days after leaving Plymouth a second time on 13th December.

Henry was not ashamed to ask for Davison's help for Harry Caltropt, the illegitimate fruit of that adventure seventeen years earlier whilst he was still celebrating his return from exile. Henry had placed Caltropt in a French Huguenot regiment - good spot for picking up the language - to add to the travails of that army in the Netherlands war. Davison was requested to watch over the lad, who was a very reluctant soldier and came to no good. "Of a bastard vine", Henry later wrote sourly, "seldom came sweet grapes". Young Harry went from bad to worse, and disappears from the picture. Miller is very critical of the treatment of the lad by a man who badly needed a son: the father's earlier indiscretion need not have been so shamefully regarded - Cecil had produced his own little grape, and Dudley was quite gentle with his.

Davison was also asked to find an office job in the Netherlands for Henry's Cornish nephew, John Michell, son of sister Jane of Truro. This boy was also living with Henry, as a servant. 'He can make copies of occurents, for though his hand be not learned, it is legible... he was wont to be called up a morning, being very given to keep his bed over long which will do him no good'. The use of the past tense suggests that Catherine had cured him of his Cornish sleeping habits.

Davison obliged. Was this the John Michell who later put his education to good use back in Cornwall receiving and distributing pirated goods?

The Killigrews were always ready to help in return, and arranged a journey to the Netherlands for Davison's wife (she was obviously more of an overseas traveller than Catherine). In gratitude for this service Mrs Davison sent back silver thread and a hunting falcon named Bon which the Killigrews found 'yet very tame and pleasant, and will not bite'.

Davison no doubt approved when Dutch Protestants received help from German Protestant Princes. English radical protestants continued to emigrate to the Netherlands in spite - or because - of the hostilities, and looked to England for political support.

English Merchant Adventurers living in Antwerp requested Davison to find them a chaplain who would conduct services according to the presbyterian model rejected so vehemently by Elizabeth. Killigrew became involved in manipulating Walter Travers into this position, the recent author of a book which had become central to the new movement. Principal Secretary Walsingham warned Harry that it would be impossible for Travers to obtain the required licence to preach abroad so Henry wove one of his sticky webs around the problem. He suggested in a letter that Davison should invite Travers over as a friend, and should then ask William Prince of Orange to request that Travers preach in the English House in Antwerp and conduct ceremonies using the local presbyterian form - so to avoid disputes with adjacent reformed churches. To avoid anticipated objections, he advised Davison to say that 'you were glad first to obtain to have one read to our nation the word of God in our own tongue which before was never yielded unto'.

If secrecy was one of the basic laws of nature in Tudor England, subterfuge was its amendment.

In April 1578, when Drake was sighting Brazil, Henry made the final plans to install Travers in the English church, and paid part of the costs of his journey. With Harry Caltropt, John Michell and Walter Travers all in the Netherlands - and Cartwright too - London must have seemed a quiet place, and the successful outcome of the Dutch war could surely only be a matter of time.

Harry undertook a short mission of military espionage to the Low Countries in 1578. His detailed report to Walsingham on the morale of local people and the strength of Spanish forces and placements has survived in the state papers. He went west again that year to convalesce from an unspecified illness, and spent ten days in Exeter.

While Drake was leading the remnant of his expedition northwards up the coast of Chile, the Elector Palatine's son Casimir, one of the German leaders involved in the Netherlands, came over to London to receive the Order of the Garter and to be banqueted by the City of London. Harry had enjoyed his company in Heidelberg nine years previously, and no doubt they renewed their acquaintance.

The English Government attempted to ally with the French and encourage them to wage war with Spain. The pro-war party remained ascendant, led by Walsingham and supported by London merchants and West Country gentry - people who had most to gain - and to lose - by challenging Philip. The holiest of wars can have a pay-off.

Following visits to Cornwall in 1577 and 1578 Henry was appointed a justice of the peace in 1579, a sign that he was anticipating fixed residence? In that year Sir Nicholas Bacon died. At his funeral at St Paul's Cathedral in March the chief mourners were Burghley, Walsingham, Master of the Rolls, Attorney General, Solicitor General, Master of the Queen's Jewel House, Sir Thomas Gresham, and brothers in law Henry Killigrew and William Cooke. He was buried in St Pauls. There is no record of Burghley trying to marry off the widowed Lady Ann.

During this year Drake worked his way northwards beyond California and then across the Pacific towards the East Indies. At the end of March 1580 he left Java, cleared the Cape of Good Hope on 18 June and regained Plymouth on 26th September.

The Queen was pleased to see Drake, and cunningly invited the French to the celebrations in his honour. The Spanish weren't going to like any of this, but Portugal had replaced Turks as a distraction. Henry, who had been appointed Surveyor of the Armoury in that year, acted as interpreter for a grand dinner at Cecil's London house, laid on for the French embassy which was caught up in Elizabeth's protracted and bogus marriage negotiations with a French prince.

In 1580 there was an outbreak of trouble near Killigrew's manor of Lanrake. He shared the tenancy of a farm with one Amy Hancock, but apparently Henry's reeve had fallen out with Amy when she insisted on ploughing and harvesting her part of the farm. What this had to do with the reeve is not clear, but Amy launched a preemptive strike onto Killigrew land accompanied by thirty men covered in plague-sores whom she had recruited in St Germans. They used a seven foot pike to send Killigrew's reeve dancing off, and lifted one hundred marks worth of corn.

The Cornish were famous for quarrelling, and anyhow violent skirmishes between neighbours were part of the daily birdsong in Elizabethan England. This episode does not appear to have attracted the conciliatory skills Henry displayed in Edinburgh, Paris, Hamburg or Blois. But he did not use the well tried do-it-yourself Killigrew-Trewynnard techniques of rural boundary maintenance. Instead the trespassers were hauled before the Court of Star Chamber.

Possibly there was more to this episode than meets the eye. Robert Hickes, the famous pirate captain, hailed from nearby Saltash, and was in cahoots with Arwennack. Was this attack on the new justice of the peace devised by Sir John as a warning to his upright brother to keep out of his affairs? Or was the whole affair a silly rustic onslaught on boredom?

From January to March 1581 the third session of the 1572 parliament was held. This was the point when, glad maybe to disabuse anyone who accused him of the worst forms of religious extremism, Henry was select to join the parliamentary committee investigating the Family of Love. After this short session, he never sat in Parliament again.

Religious behaviour was beginning to polarise, with bruised or naive believers taking the first steps towards setting up independent sects. The Catholics too were being forced into cells, and the saintly Catholic Campion was hideously racked.

Henry and Catherine had now produced four daughters - Ann, Elizabeth, Mary and Dorothy (names which have survived in common usage across the centuries) - but still no male heir for the new branch of the Killigrew family. In 1582 Catherine conceived again, although probably well into her forties (Mildred was 56) and medically frail.

In this year the French launched a naval offensive against the Spanish around the Atlantic islands of the Azores. Sir John Killigrew tried to contribute his share towards the discomfort of the Spanish, helped by his wife Lady Mary. On New Year's Day the Spanish ship Marie was driven by a wind guided with the hand of God into the safe haven of the Fal. For a week the Killigrews watched her carrying out repairs, tossing the remains of meals and raw sewerage into the river until their environmental concern took over. Then, after Sir John had diplomatically removed himself from the locality, a boat full of his servants carried out the eco-conscious assault. The Marie was robbed of its contents and carried off to Ireland, complete with its sailors, where its rubbish would do less harm to the shoreline.

Sir John convened the Commission for Piracy, whose investigations were surprisingly inconclusive, whereupon the Privy Council in London invited him to tell them what had been going on. At this time it seems that English diplomacy with Philip required a tougher line on free-lance hostilities, which was confusing for straightforward Sir John, even a little unfair. Sir John went into hiding for a while after this interview, perhaps to recover from learning that Richard Grenville was to conduct a further enquiry.

Lady Killigrew had played a considerable part in the organisation of this affair, supervising the distribution of holland cloth rifled from the ship. She was 'very ill contented' that the cargo was so disappointing. Fine leather chairs were also brought ashore, but for fear of the consequences she had these temporarily placed in casks and buried in her garden. Chairs of any sort were a rarity, her cupidity can perhaps be forgiven? Little had she in common with her devout sister in law.

During 1583 Catherine's pregnancy drew towards its term. The Killigrews probably feared the possible outcome of this confinement and prayed for divine blessing.

Catherine gave birth to a still-born child on 21st December. Her health swung in the balance over a terrible Christmas, and she died on the 27th. The father and the four girls had suffered the worst of all the possible outcomes which had been feared.

Henceforth the subdued family would have to cope without the lady of the house, and try according to the tenets of their faith to make sense of this loss, to discover what purpose it served in a cosmos where everything is predestined.

Henry and Catherine had been married for eighteen years. She was buried at the church of St Thomas the Apostle in London. Time would tell what effect this tragedy would have on Henry, now in his mid fifties. Would his whimsicality survive, or would he become one of the first of a new mutation of wizened puritans who you could see beginning to slither from the corpus of Elizabethan merchants and gentry? As a modern writer, V.S. Pritchett put it: 'puritanism gives purpose, drama and intensity to private life... Outwardly, the extreme puritan appears narrow, crabbed, fanatical, gloomy, and dull; but from the inside - what a series of dramatic climaxes his life is, what a fascinating casuistry beguiles him, how he is bemused by the comedies of duplicity, sharpened by the ingenious puzzles of the conscience, and carried away by the eloquence of hypocrisy'.

Henry seems never been like that, in spite of his eloquence. There was still important work to distract him. Events were surely going to keep him going.

ENEMIES WITHIN
AND WITHOUT

During the mid 1580s Elizabeth was busy arguing with Spain and striving for strong monarchy and national unity, but also found time to fret about religious radicalism - which she saw as a threat to her main interests. When she faced the enemy within there were the likes of Killigrew against her. When she turned again to face the enemy abroad, these enemies were clamouring to be by her side. The rigidities of the sixteenth century world-view were failing to explain these contradictions, and confusion abounded.

The Queen disliked almost any religious change, which puzzled many of her top people - who wished to raise the quality of ministry and did not share the growing desire of people like Killigrew to tamper with church services or structure. Even radicals seeking more order and government in the church scarcely whispered about new doctrine or theology.

The monarch had sent away her Archbishop in disgrace and dispensed with an appointment for several years. In 1583 Grindal died, replaced by aggressive conservative Whitgift, who on November 17th delivered his fiery inaugural sermon at St Pauls Cross: this was so close to Killigrew's house that he could have leaned from an upstairs window and thrown a Genevan tract at the new prelate.

The gauntlet Whitgift hurled was an insistence that anyone exercising an ecclesiastical function should subscribe to three articles, any of which might offend a radical. The battle of sermons raged on, with a Cambridge militant shouting defiance from St Pauls Cross in December and getting away with it. Whitgift received a mixed response to his demand for subscription to his articles, with diocesan bishops proceeding at varying speeds.

In some dioceses there were many refusals. Exeter diocese (which included Cornwall at the time) contained the least radical of clergy and preachers, and there were only three refusals compared to forty three in Essex. Ministers who petitioned the Privy Council were favourably received. The radical Robert Beale, temporary Principal Secretary during Walsingham's illness, was instructed by the Council to carry the petition to Whitgift and ask him to appear before the Council.

The intransigence of Queen and new Archbishop was forcing influential radicals into the open. Lady Ann Bacon had rarely spent time at Court but now she displayed 'earnest care and travail' for the preachers, 'resorting often unto this place to solicit those causes'.

At this point Henry Killigrew launched himself into one of his more open confrontations with an establishment figure. On May 8th he was one of twenty-five 'Kentish gentlemen' who appeared at the Archbishop's palace with a petition which the previous day they had exhibited to the Privy Council. It was led by a Kentish magnate and included prominent government servants and members of parliament, including Henry's fellow diplomat and friend Thomas Randolph (he who had complained to Cecil when Harry held up his salary) and two brothers of Catherine's mentor, the now dead Edward Dering.

Henry had no connection with Kent apart from a habit of wearing out its horses on the way to and from channel ports, so his inclusion can only have been to add weight and credibility. According to Collinson 'no episode more strikingly illustrates the contempt which the Elizabethan governing classes entertained for prelates'. Those of the delegation who were hoping that the Queen would come down on their side, given her known dislike of church barons, did not understand her deeper mistrust of radical challenges to authority, nor recognise her ability to smell from a great distance possible threats to her own sovereignty.

During June Walsingham met Whitgift and negotiated a compromise over subscription.

Henry still had a role in defending the church from other

extremists. In 1585 he worked again with Randolph. One John Meere was 'examined by Henry Killigrew and Thomas Randolph by Commission from Mr Secretary (Walsingham) in relation to his conduct towards Mrs Best. Did he use sorceries or witchcraft to trouble her with the sight of the devil?'

It perhaps demonstrates the fear of the real Devil always heaving beneath the surface of daily life that senior figures were preoccupied with such detail.

Henry continued to attend the Queen as a Gentleman of the Privy Chamber. Historian Starkey states that Killigrew was specially active as a messenger on the Queen's most intimate business. In July 1584 Leicester's cherished four year old son, the Imp, died suddenly. Grief-stricken he left the court without permission, to be with his wife. This affliction was one of a series of personal setbacks which Dudley suffered at the time. He had most earnestly wished for an heir, and had become estranged from the Queen for secretly marrying in order to achieve this.

The Queen immediately selected Henry as most appropriate to go to Leicester and his wife with a message of sympathy and symbolic forgiveness. Robert wrote back to the Queen 'whom on my knees I most humbly thank for her gracious visitation by Killigrew'. The Queen again, as with Elizabeth Hoby, responding to the anguish of bereavement with simplicity and humanity.

In 1584 a new Parliament sat, which included Killigrew brothers John and William, but not Harry, among those taking up the disproportionate number of Cornish seats; few of these were Cornishmen. Around Christmas 1585 the Killigrew's eldest daughter Anne - now about eighteen - married the promising young diplomat Henry Neville.

The wide political support for religious radicals was demonstrated in December when they were granted their request for a conference at Lambeth with their opponents. Leicester advanced the request and attended the conference, which was assisted by Burghley and Walsingham. Burghley, undoubtedly stimulated by his wife, had already taken issue with Whitgift for his 'Romish style... (like) the inquisitors of Spain'. Although its outcome was not conclusive the fact that it was held at all represented a notable symbolic victory.

Travers, whom Henry had helped to set up in Antwerp six years previously, was one of two radical leaders of the conference. Burghley had been strongly supporting him for a senior church office.

The radicals' victory was qualified however. The establishment had recently been supporting them at the expense of greater extremists and the effect was to split the movement for change. This led to enhanced fanaticism by those on the margins, which provided one major reagent for the explosive English civil war two generations later.

While these embryos of ferment were bursting out and subsiding, foreign affairs continued to preoccupy those at centre stage, with Spaniards still heading the chorus of sorcerers. French involvement in the Netherlands, ostensibly on the side of Protestants, was floundering, and Leicester led a strong political lobby for aggression against Philip. The Queen hesitated as always, gloomy about cost and pessimistic about outcome. Even Burghley, among all councillors least keen on war, recognised that unless England sent troops to the Netherlands now war would become harder to fight and disperse itself over a wider area.

During 1584 matters became more serious. After the assassination of William of Orange, the only effective Dutch protestant leader, Davison was sent to negotiate the terms of English entry to the Netherlands. Would Killigrew be dragged across in his wake?

Meanwhile at home preparations were made for a major war. The people of the West Country were being organised into local armed units, and coastal defences strengthened. Ralegh took over from Bedford as Lord Lieutenant in Cornwall, closely aided by Grenville. Strong people, big enough to deal with Arwennack. Sir John Killigrew was allowed to muster from five adjacent parishes for the defence of Pendennis Castle - an arrangement which left Penryn undefended and generated anquished complaints.

In March 1584 Sir John died - presumably unexpectedly as he left no will - owing massive sums to his brother Henry. The next John, Henry's nephew, stepped into the creaking shoes, heavy with caked estuary mud.

Henry remained closely in touch with Davison during these years. His stated desire to make a practical contribution in the Netherlands had not abated. In 1585 Spanish armies captured Antwerp, and in May definitively assaulted English interests by blockading their ships in Spanish ports. From this year onwards the English Government legally authorised reprisals on Spanish shipping: pirates for the first time acquired the more respectable status of privateers.

Burghley sought to reconcile his differences with Leicester in preparation for a likely conflict. He needed better information about Leicester's complaints about him. Elizabeth Russell was useful like Henry for having access to both the grandees. She had been sister in law to both, but was unlucky with husbands: following Hoby, Lord John Russell had died the previous year. Burghley asked her to identify the nature of Leicester's grievances against him before he wrote to propose an end to ill will. Another sister at work in the network.

The English concluded their treaty with the Netherlands in August 1585: the Queen was bound to send an army until the end of war, at her own cost - to be repaid later. Meanwhile Englishmen continued to challenge Spain in the New World. Richard Grenville planted his colony in Roanoke Island during that year - Henry acting as one of Grenville's trustees.

Young Trelawny went up to Emmanuel College, Cambridge in that year - the establishment founded by Harry's boss, Chancellor of the Exchequer Mildmay.

A leader was needed for the most substantial military expedition for many years, the army in the Netherlands. It could only be Leicester, a man who knew little about soldiering and whose leadership skills in public places had not been widely put to the test. He was commissioned to lead the army, and in December set sail with 6,000 foot and 1,000 horse.

This was not only a military expedition but would involve close political co-operation with a Dutch Council of State and its instruments and a degree of direct government. Leicester - not the humblest man or the best listener - needed trustworthy deputies and advisers committed to the Protestant cause, who understood financial as well as military matters.

It was an executive as much as a diplomatic role which Henry was asked to fill. Not far off sixty, he might have preferred to concentrate on his motherless children and keep an eye on Trelawny. Torn between conflicting duties, but with no real choice in the circumstances, his large conscience bent him towards another spell away from England.

When Leicester set off for the Netherlands he was in poor health and had recently been the subject of a lengthy and widely distributed pamphlet accusing him of an extraordinary array of unlikely crimes, one of which was to have hired William Killigrew to murder someone. The choice of William for this fictional role is interesting, because the anonymous writer knew the ins and outs of court and judged that William could credibly be planted with this crime.

The cream of English forces travelled with Leicester: senior officials, nobility and gentry who eagerly responded to his call to arms. Also a personal retinue of almost a hundred gentlemen and yeomen officers, together with their servants including chaplains, cooks and grooms. Leicester's troupe of actors and musicians. All carrying out the will of God and England under Elizabeth's banner.

Banquets and fireworks greeted the crusading English forces. On Leicester's progress through the provinces every town competed to arrange torchlit processions, decorated barges on the canals, masques. At Amsterdam there was a display of sea monsters - 'whales and others of great hugeness' were harnessed to tow his ship towards the shore.

God seemed to take time to decide whether this venture deserved fair winds. Further vessels, Burghley wrote to Leicester, were 'shipped the second day after Christmas day, all have lain at Margate in Kent ever since, to this 12. of January, for anything I can hear to the contrary, saving they have been onto the seas three or four sundry times, and put back, either with change of winds or lack of winds, and, at this present, we have had these 5 or 6 days constant easterly winds with frosts'.

Leicester was not the first outsider on whom the Netherlands' northern provinces pinned their hopes. A strong leader was needed to help them overcome differences which were threatening to destroy their chance of independence. Philip's commander, the Duke of Parma, one of the finest of the century, had toiled for eight years to subdue the southern provinces and was poised to move northwards.

Henry Killigrew was already familiar with the considerable differences between England and the Low Countries. The Netherlands was a magi's pot of all conflicts assailing northern Europe at the time. Marked contrasts in wealth, religion and politics, all spiced with treachery and violence and marionated in the threat of imminent attack.

The task for Leicester's leadership was probably impossible. A gulf existed between different interest groups: in some provinces professional and business classes had succeeded in limiting the power of fanatical Calvinists, in others Presbyterian zealots with working class support already dominated town government - countered by a Catholic minority prone to look to Spain for deliverance. Across the country individual provinces retained considerable financial autonomy, and the richer ones, mostly on the seaboard, declined to subsidise the poorer.

Leicester immediately risked the tenuous order which existed within some provinces. He tried to shift the balance of power away from merchants and professional people towards Calvinists, and to increase richer provinces' financial contributions towards the war. Henry Killigrew was required to play a leading role in this process, and also took on an important job checking the widespread fraud within the English forces, especially over payment of troops.

The English government negotiated the establishment of a Dutch Council of State as the main executive body, taking precedence over the Dutch Estates General. This Council had several Dutch members and two English advisers, one of whom was Killigrew. A Chamber of Finances was set up which attempted to discover the capacity of each province to contribute to the war, and here too Henry had a principal role.

As the complexity and intransigence of his problems began to dawn on Leicester he came to appreciate his senior aides. In February 1586, when the din from the Christmas welcome had barely subsided, Leicester wrote to Burghley: 'I have one here whom I take no small comfort in and that is little Hal Killigrew. I assure you he is a notable servant and more in him than ever I heretofore thought of him, though I always knew him to be an honest man and able'.

The English government proved as slow as the Dutch provinces to provide money for the war, and Leicester was often required to stem desertions and prevent pillaging by payments from his own pocket.

The town of Utrecht became the centre of Leicester's operations. Here Calvinists formed a strong force committed to uniting northern provinces by replacing existing town rulers with a Protestant elite. Naturally this did not go down well in other places, especially the sea-board provinces such as Holland, rich from trade and smuggling with Spain whom they were supposed to be fighting.

Leicester only managed to undertake one major campaign. Some provinces were even unwilling to garrison English troops in case this led to attacks. When the town of Deventer refused to allow the entry of troops, Killigrew was sent to keep the town council busy for two days with protracted discussions while English soldiers filtered into the town disguised as citizens.

Once three hundred men were secretly concealed within the walls the English commander felt confident to demand an answer on official troop-entry by the following morning. Before they took to their beds, the town worthies trebled the watch and threw chains across the streets to prevent the troops. Early next morning the advance guard of filtered troops emerged from their hiding places and formed up in the market place. Their commander disbanded the town guard and imprisoned the councillors.

Harry clashed with the leader of Holland province, Paul Buys, who was resisting probes into the finances of this rich part of the country. Killigrew threatened that Leicester 'would establish the Chamber of Finances or risk his neck... order would be taken with Buys for his course and practices were too well-known'.

Leicester soon began to support Calvinist attempts to subvert the commercially rich seaboard provinces. A coup d'état was engineered in Utrecht, during which Killigrew gave strong support to Calvinist street leaders. Leicester's partisans arrested and imprisoned Buys in Utrecht in July 1586.

As a result of this dissipation of military energy in the north, the Anglo-Dutch alliance made little headway against the Spanish in the south. A successful encounter with the Spanish at Zutphen near Deventer was overshadowed by the death there of Sir Philip Sidney.

A great deal of money was wasted and many among the Dutch doubted English intention to fight Spain, suspecting instead that Elizabeth was using the presence of her forces as a bargaining lever to make peace with Philip and prevent invasion of England. Trust was not a strong currency in sixteenth century England, and Elizabeth's Machiavellian ways were well known.

In November 1586, less than a year after Robert Dudley's triumphal entry, the Queen realised she needed him more at home than abroad, and replaced him as overall commander. Comforting little Hal returned too - his loyalty had been impressive, but was it well judged? Would tougher opposition to Leicester by his advisers have been in everyone's interest? Killigrew was surely thoroughly disillusioned by this demonstration of protestant radicalism, in sharp contrast to Huguenot campaigns in France, and he probably hoped never to see the Low Countries again.

PHILIP'S PERSONAL DISASTER

On his return to England Harry was immediately caught in the climactic struggle to persuade one Divinely Appointed Queen to execute Another. Elizabeth keenly appreciated the contradiction inherent in her dilemma. God could only be on one side, but Mary *was* a kinswoman. The killing of Monarchs was a habit which could spread if encouraged.

As with all Elizabethan conflict, this was not a matter of merely seeking political advantage. In the public mind Mary was seen as Evil's hot bed-fellow, capable of poisoning every well.

Mary had been the centre of attention by dint of encapsulating the twin problems of Scottish security and the English succession: now eyes were being deflected towards Spain's every move and patience was in short supply. Walsingham had successfully trapped Mary whilst locked in her English prison into giving conclusive evidence of plotting with Philip. This treachery at a time of maximum national peril forced reluctant Elizabeth to sanction the death.

At the final hour Elizabeth hesitated, and having signed the death warrant she tried to delay, but was too late. A complicated series of messages and orders had already been set in motion and Mary was beheaded in February 1587 at the castle of Fotheringay. Henry was one of the emissaries, the principal messenger was his friend Davison. The Queen dropped into one of her troughs of self-deception and rage, and sought to shift the blame onto others. Disgraced and deprived of office, Davison was imprisoned in the Tower. Henry barely escaped blame.

The Tower! That damp college of statecraft which had apprenticed

Elizabeth herself, Dudley, Cecil, Cooke, Throckmorton. Henry must have glanced at the place narrowly while his friend was there, and remembered Pendennis, Rouen, Edinburgh. So far he had evaded its shadows.

Mary was mourned by few in a country acutely aware of national interests and danger from Spain. In a period when celebrating heroes served the cause of unity, Sidney's state funeral at St Pauls was the first ever accorded to someone not brimful of royal blood. Henry joined Leicester in trying to comfort Walsingham over the loss of his widely loved son-in-law. Dudley had written from the Netherlands: 'what perfection he was grown unto and how able to serve her majesty and his country... I have lost, beside the comfort of my life, a most principal stay and help in my service here'.

Genuinely or to buy time, the Queen and Council endeavoured to persuade Spain of their interest in peace. Meanwhile Cornwall was inevitably caught up in the preparations to resist the onslaught of the Armada and - if necessary - to take the war onto enemy coasts and shipping.

Grenville returned from escorting colonists to north America and reviewed local bands of trained soldiers. Drake slipped out on the famous voyage to destroy much of the Armada in preparation, bringing back a hugh East Indies carrack, the San Felipe, full of silks, spices and jewels. Sir Francis Godolphin (and perhaps his wife, who as a Killigrew would surely not stay at home on such occasions) journeyed past Lanrake to Saltash, where he made an inventory of the contents, marvelling at the heaps of gold, pendants, rings, stones 'which we esteem to be garnets', the 'agates small and great, and other stones of a green colour with spots of red'.

Among the many ships contributed by the West Country to the fleet which prepared to meet the Armada was the 'John Trelawny', supplied by Saltash and Tavistock, 150 tons and 30 men.

Arwennack as before could not get it quite right. In 1587 John Killigrew the Third imprisoned and robbed a Danish merchant ship which had taken refuge in the harbour of the Fal to escape a French pirate. England was certainly not in the business of antagonising a country with whom it was keen to develop trade and political co-operation. Killigrew was ordered to pay compensation to this neutral vessel but failed to do so: the Privy Council, among other matters of more importance, ordered his arrest.

Henry's nephew 'fleeteth from place to place' - which must have been a relief to Penryn - and the Council wondered whether a writ of rebellion could be issued against him. He was accompanied by an armed retinue, and though sheriffs pleaded that they sought him in vain the Privy Council were reluctant to believe their excuses. Eventually Uncle Henry paid the gigantic sum of £445 to the defrauded Danish merchant 'to pacify her Majesty's anger and to save the castle (of Pendennis) from forfeiture and himself (John) from prison'.

Killigrew - close to spy-masters Burghley, Walsingham and Leicester - must have been heavily engaged in counter-espionage during these months, most of it concealed, unrecorded and nasty. A shred of evidence survives in a Privy Council instruction on 24th April 1587 from Burghley, Walsingham and others - a letter to Sir Owen Hopton (Lieutenant of the Tower), Thomas Randolph, Henrie Killigrew and Richard Yonge that 'whereas one Andreas van Metter, prisoner in the Tower, stood charged with certain matters concerning her Majesty's state and person which he did obstinately refuse to confess, their Lordships require them, if he should still persist in his said obstinacy, to use the accustomed torture of the racke as often times as they should see cause, to force him to confess what might be had out of him touching the said matters'.

This letter must have referred to a matter of high security, no mere Dutch sea-captain trading illegally with Spain. The official sanction of 'accustomed torture' - the term is used without equivocation - follows its concealed use by Burghley during the Ridolphi affair. The cause of nation and religion were deemed to be the justification, but there is little evidence that the rack was ever requested with any relish.

Widowed sixty year old Killigrew - released from the deadening frustration of a failed overseas commission to skin the Dutch elite, enraged at one Queen's treachery but also by another Queen's vile treatment of his friend in that same Tower and by her persecution of his religious allies, pestered by his cretinous Cornish nephew - not a happy a man during early 1587, his intimate life perhaps set aside as he sailed alone with the wind of war, not overscrupulous with the sinews and joints of van Metters?

Henry's desire to enjoy the spring with his family was also forcefully shattered. Parma was ordered by Philip to shift his operations to the coast. Here he should join the huge Armada soon to sail from Spain, and stand ready to attack - or at least pretend to attack - the mainland of England. To meet this challenge the Queen ordered an enhanced English effort in the Low Countries, led again by Leicester.

The Queen summoned Henry to Greenwich where he was once more appointed to serve the less than successful Dutch Council of State. His fellow councillor this time was his old acquaintance Robert Beale, Walsingham's brother in law, who three years earlier had taken a leading role in mobilising the Privy Council's stand against Whitgift: two leading members of a specialising inner circle, radical protestants in power.

Leicester crossed in June 1587 with 3,000 fresh troops and a flotilla under Admiral Lord Howard. Killigrew and Beale helped to plan renewed efforts against Spain: essential Dutch co-operation was consistently refused, leaving Leicester as exposed and unsuccessful as before. Dutch politicians in the Council of State were convinced that Elizabeth was treating with Spain: attempts to raise money for the war failed and ships were withheld.

By October Killigrew had accepted that Leicester had come to the end of a very flat road in the Low Countries. The attempt to use the Council of State as the main instrument of government could not succeed. 'Men who wish you best', he wrote to Leicester, 'say it is time for a conference between you and the states. I think it is a better way than by striving'.

Leicester returned to England in December: he required Henry, who hoped to return too, to stay as the chief English representative on the Council of State. Harry wrote despairingly to Walsingham: 'I hope this may be no hindrance to my revocation, which I beseech you to hasten, as you love me'. The duty in the Netherlands may have seemed little better than the fate of his able and loyal friend Davison, locked in the Tower.

Killigrew now had to serve up the Queen's shift from a policy of junket setting to cheese making, and to walk away from Calvinist militants towards leading sea-board merchants who dominated the States General. Henry was tainted with rennet from his contact with Leicester: 'I perceive myself not to be the best welcome among them'. They talked in Dutch over his head, slighting his reputation as a considerable linguist. Nonetheless the States General were no more successful than Leicester or others before him in uniting the Netherlands against the Spanish, or in controlling unruly soldiers. The milk seemed too sour for any purpose. Henry became increasingly suspicious that the States General were aiming to crush those still loyal to the alliance, drive out the English - even by attacking their forces - and make their own peace with Spain.

In March 1588 Elizabeth, seeking her habitual consensus, ordered Killigrew and the new English commander to persuade all the factions, including Calvinist partisans, to support the States General. Henry wrote to Leicester expressing his distaste at abandoning his former partners. While he sent home useful intelligence about the build-up of Parma's forces in the south, he reluctantly implemented the new politics with some success. By summer, with minds wonderfully concentrated by imminence of the Armada, the northern provinces were rolled into a ball of unity.

His West Country brethren were ready when the Armada appeared. In full vestments the Catholic fleet processed up the Channel: the English ships followed like a flock of rebellious choir boys with tapers lit, and when the time was right they plunged their fire into the heart of orthodoxy. God seems to have sent a larger wind across the sea.

When the English and Spanish navies engaged at the end of July Henry was still negotiating with the Dutch. He sent home further intelligence reports about the sea-battle and its outcome of improved relations with the Dutch. However, during this summer he was often ill and letters pleading for recall became frequent.

In September, when the remains of the Armada still crawled into confessional corners, Leicester died - a tired and unjustly treated man with few friends. Henry, who had been slow to leave the Dudley household when John fell in 1553, thirty-five years on wrote to Walsingham for leave to attend the funeral of Robert, 'that I may yield him the last service and testimony of my devotion'.

In that month too, Parma led his forces against the Anglo-Dutch garrison at Bergen-op-Zoom, an important trading centre. Killigrew now threw all his weight behind Dutch appeals for further military support to the garrison from England '...lest they quail before the fiery sword of the Duke of Parma'. The Queen acted swiftly to send a considerable force and Parma was required to make a humiliating withdrawal. Miller comments: 'the legend of Spanish invincibility on land had been shattered just as that of its supremacy on the seas had been destroyed the previous summer'. That provides one way of looking at the affair, but had Philip not shown that he could mass two huge forces within sight of England, and might always try again - hoping for a different lee shore?

Henry still felt he had to knock the swallows' nest out of the rafters in the milk-parlour. Some parts of the Netherlands, including Utrecht which he had earlier helped to subvert, continued to hold out against the States General. Henry was keen to clear up resistance, linking this with earning his return home. In October he wrote 'the controversies for which it pleased Her Majesty to continue my service here the longer are all appeased save this new brabble at Utrecht'. The brabble was soon resolved.

In England, in spite of their victory, fatigue and confusion blanketed the Government and its leaders. The Queen remained divinely right, shifting blame for all difficulties. Burghley wrote to Walsingham in November 'all resolutions and lacks are thrown upon us two in all her speeches to everybody. The wrong is intolerable'.

Henry's tribute to Burghley in the autumn reflected that weariness which afflicted the governors of England. Even the style of the letter creaks on, although that had often been Hal's way. 'It grieveth me who have no means but by prayer to relieve by any service of mine the least part of the cares you have for the steering of that ship, wherein God hath appointed you to be a pilot from the beginning, that so many storms hath threatened shipwreck and to pilot... against all the power and practice of the wicked, as I trust He will do still, and to bring you and yours long home, even to Himself (in his time), and that in peace'.

In January 1589, a little over three years since Leicester's spectacular arrival, Henry left the incomprehensible Dutch to their own whey-tub. The war with Spain would continue for many years, and the ambiguities of England's attempt to ally with a Protestant anti-colonial rebellion would doubtless reinforce the Queen's doubts about a grand anti-Catholic alliance. Although things had never been simple in Havre, Edinburgh or Heidelberg, Killigrew too may have soured to Dutch Protestants.

If England required more exciting use of language than Killigrew's, happily Shakespeare had recently arrived in London. In the display of fresh religious and political energies would any role be found on stage for this or that old Cornish Polonius?

HENRY AND JAÉL OF LOTHBURY.

A t a little over sixty, according to the standards of the age Harry was already an old man in 1589. Mildred Cecil died in that year, and with Hoby, Bacon and Russell all dead, none of the great Cooke marriages survived.

Burghley boasted about the number of aristocrats who turned out for his wife's send-off, with its carefully planned procession of three hundred and fifteen mourners.

Henry's network seemed to be failing. Following Leicester, Walsingham died in 1590, so poor from financing national security out of his own pocket that his body was buried by night to avoid attentions from his creditors. Davison was in disgrace. Lately radical Protestantism had no champion in high places.

England's relations with its neighbours were stable for a while, following the defeat of the Armada. Now, it might be expected, would be the hour for little Hal to retire from his offices and limp off to enjoy his Cornish estate, relapsing perhaps into a widower's cruel nostalgia and self-absorption. But Henry had two French affairs ahead of him, one of the heart and the other political.

It can only have caused astonishment when rumours proposed that he was heading towards another marriage - confirmed when in 1590 he arrived once more in St Peter le Poor to marry. Frenchwoman Jaél de Peigne was twenty five years or more his junior. Catherine had died trying to bring him a boy, the old man steadied himself outside the church and departed with Jaél to sire three sons and a daughter.

In this year too the Killigrews moved house, acquiring a substantial property in Lothbury, an area where brother William lived too, just north of today's Bank of England. At the time Lothbury rivalled Bishopgate to be the City's most fashionable area - millionaires' rows of tall half timbered houses. Perhaps Jaél wanted to shift a little from Cooke's ghosts. Or perhaps Henry was tiring of conservative religious invective thundering from St Paul's Cross following a celebrated sermon by prelate Bancroft in February 1589.

Whatever the motive for the move they probably left the Churchyard with relief. The air inside St Pauls was not scented with deep spirituality; the church had become a roadstead for cutpurses and pimps who pirated on gullible rural gentry parading in newly acquired finery. Around the building stalls of booksellers were vending every kind of political and religious invective, both above and below the counter, including copies of Marprelate Tracts attacking the established church. You had to be careful if you wanted to purchase anti-Government propaganda at St Pauls: if you bought from agents provocateurs who plied proscribed material you were hauled off for questioning, perhaps by Killigrew.

Harry's brother was involved with the local church of St Margaret's, and regularly gave money to it, but Henry does not seem to have been interested, possibly attending with Jaél the London Huguenot church which he later endowed in his will.

Surely the change in London life most noticeable to Henry on his return from the Netherlands was the decline and retreat of the radical religious movement. In 1590 several leaders including Henry's confederate Cartwright were imprisoned for nothing worse than refusing to co-operate with Whitgift's unconstitutional ecclesiastical commission. Elizabeth Russell corresponded defiantly with the Archbishop.

The death of Leicester proved to be crucial. Like Killigrew, he had accepted not only new attitudes to preaching and the Bible but also the latest notions of Calvinist church order - elected ministers who shared authority with lay elders. This type of presbyterianism was now forging ahead in France, Scotland and the Netherlands but was not found in the vision of earlier radical leaders like Dering, nor figured in the compromise between Walsingham and Whitgift.

Henry Killigrew can only have been dismayed when counter-attacks by the established church gathered force. However, he would have noted that many of the tenets of radical Protestants were becoming absorbed into mainstream church culture: the decline of organised radicalism was partly due to its success as a climate of opinion, and the movement could only continue around principles and practices requiring greater innovation, such as independent sectarianism.

Hostility from the Queen, effective resistance by new members of the Privy Council, loss of key influence at Court, indifference of the great majority of churchgoers to further religious change, recognition of sharp intolerance practised by a growing number of fundamentalists (which became so evident sixty years later in the Civil War), these all explain why presbyterianism and sectarianism failed to achieve the headway being made in some neighbouring countries.

If there were still a few people close to the centre of power who might have offered leadership by at least protecting Presbyterian ideals, if not actively advancing them, one was Henry Killigrew. His apparent failure to do so may have been caused by advancing age, family preoccupations, continued work on foreign policy, or a keener eye for hectoring and bullying potential within presbyterianism evident during his time in the Netherlands. Or could his quietude have signalled a loss of courage and commitment?

A further and perhaps decisive reason prompting Henry's withdrawal from active leadership of religious fundamentalists is likely to have been the increasingly more obvious threat they posed to his class - the successful gentry. In 1590 Walsingham had described - in a letter perhaps drafted by Henry's nephew Francis Bacon - how the radical cause was losing its appeal to the propertied classes. "But now of later years, when there issued from them (some) that affirmed the consent of the magistrate was not be attended; when ... they combined themselves by classes and subscriptions; when they descended into that vile and base means of defacing the government of the Church by ridiculous pasquils (lampoons); when they began to make many subjects in doubt to take oaths, which is one of the fundamental parts of justice in this land, and in all places...; then it appeared to be no more conscience but mere faction and division'.

This dilemma - the need to choose between religious ideals and property interests - came to a head in the English civil war fifty years later: Henry Killigrew's own son embodied this, speaking out sympathetically in King Charles' Parliament for radical change but eventually siding with Royalists and dying from wounds sustained at the siege of (true enough) Pendennis Castle. The next generation of Cornish Godolphins were divided between the two sides during the Civil War.

Yet Elizabeth and Whitgift could not prevent a few frigates of church reform from beating on to windward, especially as the invisible tide was so firmly in their favour. In the late eighties the radical movement had instigated a series of enquiries into the state of clergy in each county, and around 1593 the findings of these registers began to filter through, although not all were published. Lady Ann Bacon, who was using the Bacon estate at Gorhambury in Hertfordshire as one of the few safe houses for religious radicals, contributed to distribution of this material.

The register for Cornwall undoubtedly exaggerates and sometimes falsifies, but it cannot all have been lies. Clergy include the best wrestler in Cornwall, a common gamester, a lewd drunkard, a good archer, a bad hireling (lately a button maker), and one who became a minstrel. One was a good dicer and carder, both night and day, and one 'keepeth a whore and hath had five or six bastards'. Another had lately married a common harlot.

Ann Bacon's continuing fight required circumspection. Writing to her elder son Anthony she advised him to burn her letter. 'Beware liberal speeches these suspicious days... biting vipers the whole part of them'. Francis noted that a wise man always reserved 'a window open to fly out or some secret back-door for retreat'.

Beale gave warning 'not to addict yourself to any faction that you may find among the councillors. You shall find they will only use you for their own turns and that done will set little by you afterwards'.

Foreign affairs continued to preoccupy the nervous government. Defeat of the Armada was really only the beginning of a war which spilt on for well over a decade. In 1589 Drake was one leader of an officially sanctioned joint stock expedition to Portugal which included again the 'John Trelawny'. Jonathan Trelawny himself may have profited from fitting out and provisioning these ships, but the expedition failed.

Sir Francis Godolphin as deputy lieutenant received instructions for Cornwall's role in tightening the sea blockade of Spain. Innumerable ships were brought into the Fal River and other harbours to be examined. Neutral ships were allowed to pass unless cargos appeared to be contraband, in which case goods were sold and war material reserved for the government. It was particularly important to stop illegal corn and equipment for ships.

The town which eventually became Falmouth grew at this time, profiting from war, but in 1589 John Killigrew was deprived of his position as a vice-admiral of Cornwall. He was either unable or unwilling to fortify Pendennis Castle, and so could offer no resistance to later Spanish attacks on the coastline. However he was not replaced as governor of the castle until 1598, thereby ending fifty six years of continuous governorship by his family.

And Henry Killigrew's second French affair? The Armada had been defeated but Spaniards had shown themselves capable of putting a huge force to sea and taking it up the length of the English Channel. Within two years they possessed a new fleet of 100 ships totalling 43,000 tons. When they invaded France to join the strong pro-Spanish element there, the new French King leading the Protestant anti-Spanish element was compelled to ask Elizabeth for money to continue the war. England too was broke and to provide a loan of £20,000 the Council had to raid the coffers of the Tellers of the Exchequer. Henry Killigrew had £9,000 available and the rest came from other Tellers - angels, francs, pistolets and ninety bags of silver.

The Spanish were short of money too, due in part to success of English sailors in attacking treasure ships from the New World. In 1591 Philip arranged for a fleet to be sent westwards across the Atlantic for the proper protection of his convoy: the fleet encountered an English naval force in the Azores, and in the ensuing fight Sir Richard Grenville in The Revenge sustained his famous fight and lost his life. His cousin Ralegh wrote a powerful defence of Richard's performance.

During 1590 and 1591 the English were sending soldiers to boost anti-Spanish forces in France. In August 1591 3,600 troops were sent to Dieppe en route for another relief of Rouen. The commander was the brave but unreliable Earl of Essex, twenty-six years old survivor of the Netherlands War and step-son of the Earl of Leicester.

The Queen wanted Essex to be guided and restrained; scanning for experienced advisers she noted Harry avoiding eye contact. A man in his sixties with a young wife and dynastic anxieties had different considerations. Others had succeeded in dodging this draft, and Essex had objected to some names including one of the Russells. Henry pleaded infirmity but the Queen was short of wise old counsellors in this time of peril: she insisted that bridling a headstrong Earl would be service of mind rather than body - a job which lame dull comforting little Hal could manage.

The other adviser was Sir Thomas Leighton - who with Henry had sought to relieve Rouen against the Queen's orders almost thirty years previously and finished up in the same prison. How comical and touching the haunting by these two old spectres from a previous generation of war. Had they not tried, as Essex will try now, to stalk out the boundaries of the permissible in that very theatre?

Essex took many friends to France, including eighteen year old Henry Wriothsley, Earl of Southampton, soon to become Shakespeare's famous patron. As Burghley had been Southampton's guardian Killigrew would have known the propensities of this troublesome young aristocrat.

At this time Killigrew was one of a handful mentioned as likely to succeed Walsingham in the post of Principal Secretary; the rehabilitation of Davison was also considered. However the vacant Principal Secretaryship became a crucial battleground in the growing rivalry between Burghley and Essex.

The efforts of Essex to gain supremacy at Court were beginning to alarm the Queen. Unlike Dudley and Burghley of a previous generation, he was not content to dominate one of two balanced spheres of influence. To counter his increasingly wild ambitions the Queen supported Burghley's efforts to keep the Secretaryship open until his son Robert Cecil was ready for it.

From now until the execution of Essex the enmity between Cecil and Essex dominated politics. Harry Killigrew had been unusual in remaining a trusted member of both Cecil's and Dudley's networks. Would he now try to maintain balanced relations with both sides of the much more bitter conflict at centre stage?

Killigrew's dilemma would probably surface whilst he was in France. He had clearly been posted by Elizabeth and Burghley, but if he wanted to continue to span two major factions he would have to find ways to keep in with increasingly powerful Essex without compromising his integrity. However Essex did not usually play hard to get: if he judged Harry to be a valuable person he would seek to join him to his sphere of influence, or at least he might try to encourage the much older man to be neutral or even-handed. Either way he would probably smooth Harry's way to an accommodation.

In France there existed only quite limited scope for two elderly advisers seeking to influence the determined and not entirely coherent Essex and his military command. But if Henry was true to form he might try to be honest broker.

If the Queen thought that Harry could now be considered politically correct she was in for another of her disappointments. Soon Burghley was writing on her behalf to Killigrew and Leighton upbraiding them for encouraging Essex to action. If Henry thought the language of his tickings off might now be less imperious, he was wrong too: "the more she thought about it, the greater she found the fault and the more necessary that they understand so from her own letters".

Whether or not as a result of this letter, Killigrew fell ill and Leighton suffered great pain from gout. The Queen, as always impatient for outcomes and worried about cost, soon demanded the return of Essex, although Killigrew and others sought to dissuade her. Under pressure she agreed to let some troops stay under command of ghost Leighton: however, Leighton and Killigrew were ordered to ensure Essex did not hear about this concession until after he had sailed home, in case he should defy her orders (she had already got the measure of him). In the event circumstances changed and Essex was allowed to stay for several months more.

Henry did not join action during this mission, remaining in Dieppe where he had once dried out after a disastrous storm at sea. He acted as link between the army before Rouen and the government at home, also supervising pay and provisions of soldiers. Citizens of Dieppe were no keener on English troops than the people of Deventer had been, although they would explain their hostility by referring to looting and desecration carried out by foreigners. The French often left English sick or wounded to die in streets and fields. Twice Killigrew paid substantial amounts of his own money to obtain food for the wounded and ships to allow them to be returned home. The Queen complained that arrival of disease-ridden troops in English ports threatened to spread the plague.

In November the famous Cornish veteran made the hazardous journey to Rouen, no doubt remembering points on the way. He arrived safely. An eye-witness reported that on 20th November Essex 'rose very early and... accompanied with my Lord Ambassador and many others, he alighted on a fair green and so did many others, not knowing his intent, and there he knighted Sir Henry Killigrew'.

That it had taken so long for Henry to receive this honour had no special significance. Elizabeth had been notoriously mean with all rewards - there was a similar delay in recognising the remarkable career of John Hawkins. Later Essex came to cheapen knighthoods in his bid to enhance his own faction, and was forbidden to continue the practice, but at this point the award would have carried considerable prestige, especially in Cornwall where it signalled the founding of a new dynasty branching from an otherwise failed family.

Soon afterwards Killigrew sailed home, arriving in time for Christmas. He may have found Cecil a little frosty towards him. Shortly behind him came Essex and Southampton. Around this time Shakespeare entered the Southampton circle: if Sir Harry Killigrew did not meet him in the big houses he probably saw him acting with the Chamberlain's Men.

Killigrew's daily routine peeps through fragments of surviving documentation, suggesting that his role as an unofficial state inquisitor continued. In January 1592 members of the Star Chamber including the Archbishop, the Lord Treasurer, Chancellor of the Exchequer Fortescue (Henry's neighbour in Hendon) and Robert Cecil wrote to Sir Henry Killigrew, Robert Beale, Sergeant Fleetwood (the harsh and humorous Recorder of London), Richard Yonge (Henry's fellow torturer of 1587) and others, asking them in groups of three to examine Jesuits and other Catholics who had been imprisoned as suspects and were long-time unexamined.

Three inquisitors at a time, one perhaps to keep a special look-out for the Devil.

In April 1592 another privateering English squadron, financed by the Queen, Ralegh and London merchants, captured the Madre de Dios of 1,600 tons and brought it back to Plymouth with an escort of love-sick cuttlefish and a cargo estimated at £800,000. William Killigrew was appointed a commissioner to ensure the Queen received her due share of the spoils. Events overtook the commissioners and even Robert Cecil and Ralegh - the latter released from prison for the purpose - could do nothing to prevent English seamen making off with goods from the moored ship to sell at knock-down prices. Plymouth reeked of cinnamon, cloves and musk. Cecil wrote to his father that he could smell the town from Exeter.

In June the Star Chamber wrote a letter to Sir Henry Killigrew, Sir Michael Blount and William Waad (Clerk of the Council - later a particularly mean persecutor of Ralegh) instructing them to examine Duffield, sea captain, lately committed to the Tower.

England's enemies not only committed directly hostile acts but also attempted to weaken parts of the nation indirectly by spreading destabilising or demoralising rumour. In April 1593 another official letter to Henry and others asked them 'to examine by secret means' who may be authors of libels suggesting that violence was about to be unleashed against foreign artisans.

Killigrew, once diplomat, Exchequer official and colonial administrator, was now among a core who formed the vital ganglion in the jumpy brain of state security. But he still had time for more agreeable intimacies.

OUT OF ENGLAND

1544	Scotland (?)
1549	Italy
1554-7	France
1556	Italy
1557	Strasbourg
1558	France, Heidelberg, Stuttgart
1559	France (twice)
1560	Scotland
1562-3	France (twice)
1566	Scotland (twice)
1567	Scotland
1569	Germany
1571-2	France
1572	Scotland
1573	Scotland
1574	Scotland
1575	Scotland
1578	Netherlands
1585-6	Netherlands
1587-9	Netherlands
1591	France

NOISE AND SILENCE

In 1592 Henry and Jaél Killigrew celebrated the birth of their first son, Joseph. Peals of bells celebrating this event added to the clamour which was winding England up for the last and perhaps most frenzied outbreak of Tudor paranoia.

Henry continued to demonstrate his capacity to locate kinsmen and confederates among the new faces in top places. Essex remained the Queen's favourite and it would be some years before he embarked on the unbalanced and self-destructive acts which led to his execution. One would expect Harry to have strengthened his links with the young Earl by now. This kind of calculation may have influenced the moves made by Killigrew's son-in-law Henry Neville to become an important member of the Essex grouping.

Others were moving more emphatically towards Essex, notably Francis Bacon, nephew of both Burghley and Killigrew. Although Francis was a Cooke, in later years he became the writer and philosopher who showed most impatience with the conservative thinking of the Elizabethan era, including in his line of fire the Cambridge philosophy which had inspired the Cookes.

The Queen continued to reinforce the strength of the Cecils. Burghley lived on and maintained his influence until 1598, but increasingly it was Robert who took the reigns of power to balance Essex as Cecil had countered Dudley.

The life of London burst with a new tone and style which must have seemed deeply unfamiliar to men of Sir Harry's generation. Fashions in clothing soared up over the top, theatres were defying puritans. Shakespeare was beginning to make his name with his poems: in 1593 and 1594 Venus and Adonis and The Rape of Lucrece were published by a printer in Blackfriars, one of London's calm oases where Ann Bacon and Elizabeth Russell lived and which Killigrew and Shakespeare must have visited. The poems were sold at the White Greyhound in St Paul's Churchyard.

Shakespeare may not have taken to the old Cooke sisters and their double double toil and trouble. A few years later Elizabeth Russell was among thirty inhabitants of Blackfriars who petitioned the Privy Council because Burbage, Shakespeare's associate, had bought rooms there and was converting them into a common playhouse. This development threatened to prove a great annoyance to the neighbourhood, as vagrant and lewd persons would gather on pretence of coming to plays. And playhouse being near church, trumpets and drums would disturb divine service. Did this protest derive only from religious conviction, or betray concern for house prices?

The playhouse went elsewhere. The Globe might otherwise have been in Blackfriars.

Many in the population shared the Queen's dislike of the latest religious fundamentalism. 1593 was a year of marked attack on sects operating completely outside the established church, and saw the first executions of separatists. Some victims were fanatics, others saintly and reflective individuals striving to do without hierarchies, whose spiritual descendants two generations later would sound the first heart-beats of Quakerism.

Lady Russell wrote somewhat disingenuously to Robert Cecil, hoping to secure the appointment of James Morice, radical Attorney of the Court of Wards, to membership of the Council Board. She longed for a return to 'the maintenance of the state by the laws of the realm and not by rigour'. Parliamentarians were being punished merely for challenging the arrogant ecclesiastical commission and corrupt use of church courts. Morice had recently spent two months in confinement for his attack in parliament on church courts; when he introduced two bills - for abolition of oaths and against unlawful imprisonment - he was deprived of office, suspended from practising as a lawyer and imprisoned for several years in Tutbury Castle. The Queen was behind her archbishop. Shakespeare did not need to cast back to King Henry the Eighth for a model of arbitrary sovereignty.

The Queen's impatience with religious extremists was caused partly by her continuing anxiety about the war with Spain, which continued on many fronts including France, the Netherlands and increasingly Ireland. Francis Godolphin became the only Englishmen in the history of the country to face an assault by Spaniards on English soil. At the end of July 1595 a party of Spanish descended on Mousehole, Newlyn and Penzance in south-west Cornwall. Francis happened to be in the area but locals were unwilling to respond to his calls for resistance, at least until they had taken time to think about the matter. Pendennis had been too run down by Henry's nephew to supply effective retaliation.

Henry does not seem to have been a regular visitor to Cornwall during these years. He was in London during the early summer of 1594, when the rain it raineth ev'ry day, in order to receive Carew and Trelawny with their petition about land tenure. In this highly charged atmosphere Queen and Councillors were keen to find a way to stabilise the Cornish.

His health may have been failing at this time. In May he gave over his suit to be Receiver of the Court of Wards, which it was said the Queen was intending to give to him.

At nearly seventy - a tremendous old age in that era - Sir Harry was still in demand for foreign diplomacy. In the autumn of 1595 the Queen appointed him as an envoy to the King of France but illness prevented his departure. At this time he lived for a while with his brother in Lothbury, where he was 'sorely tormented with a sore eye, and cannot read and write'. He was drafted with Beale and rehabilitated Davison to take part in negotiations for debt repayment with his old sparring partners in the Netherlands States General.

Killigrew continued to receive requests for use of his influence with others in high office. He had received a letter in 1594 from William Treffry of Fowey in Cornwall, thanking him for several services. Help to Treffry did not end there. In 1595 Elizabeth and the Lord Keeper went through the lists of Justices of the Peace and weeded some out according to judgments of their quality. Sometimes these judgments must have been wrong, or perhaps caused too much loss of face. Henry wrote - or perhaps dictated - to Robert Cecil using his characteristic style, rambling and a little obscure like a Cornish lane: "It pleased your Honour to favour my cousin, this bearer's brother, William Treffry, as to procure him to be a Commissioner of Peace in Cornwall. Since, as I understand from these assizes, he is left out of the Commission by direction of the Lord Keeper, to his no small disgrace and our discredits. I know the gentleman to be of very sufficient living, of sound religion, and learning and judgment to execute such authority, and no Justice to the west of his house within thirty miles, nor to the north within twelve, nor to the east within six; the town where he dwelleth (Fowey) being a place subject to many disorders through the common recourse of men of war to that harbour, I am bold to desire your honour to be a means to the Lord Keeper for his re-establishment, as well in regard to her Majesty's better service in that shire, as to salve the credit of the gentleman."

John Killigrew the Third had now almost destroyed the family's main branch. In that year he had tipped off an English pirate who lurked around the Fal river in Spain's service, enabling the man to escape from the Crown's searches: John was rewarded with nine bolts of holland cloth. He was called to London to account for this and other misdeeds, and travelled the path of self-justification well trodden by his father and grandfather. Unlike them he had never managed to ride the mule of government ambiguity about piracy. He was also pulled up that year for his debts, which included £1,700 to the Queen and £10,000 to moneylenders - massive sums in those days. He owed a substantial amount to his uncle Hal, whose claim he foolishly declared was fraudulent. Henry submitted an account to the government listing Arwennack debts stretching back thirty seven years, which amounted to £1,879.3s.6d, without reckoning interest.

John eventually spent much of his time in London prisons. Because the force of law and order was now firmly established, piracy was no longer commercially viable but required bribery on too widespread a scale.

The nation benefited from the demise of piracy, privateering and speculative if legitimate enterprises such as Ralegh's. The historian

Bindoff systematically catalogued their down-side. "At a time when the country was short of capital for peaceful enterprise, they diverted considerable quantities of capital to sterile or destructive ends. At a time when international credit was making patient headway in the face of ignorant hostility, they dealt its delicate mechanism wanton and damaging blows. And at a time when economic thought was beginning to outgrow its age-long preoccupation with the precious metals, they pandered to the fatal lure of gold and silver and gave bullionism a new lease of life'. The official use of privateers discouraged the development of a proper navy. Widespread piracy led to commercial monopolies: 'the unsafety of the high seas raised freights, hindered small enterprise, necessitated government protection, justified a system of licences, and so led on to restriction and large protectionist trading companies'.

Henry had found his own ways of making money, including no doubt accepting the customary sweeteners which smoothed palms of people who smoothed paths. He did not only adopt the causes of the well-to-do. In August 1598 he wrote to the High Judge of the Admiralty Court on behalf of a Cornish constable who was being required to pay charges for allowing a thief to escape.

He also helped the Crown in its efforts to stay solvent. In 1598 the Privy Council wrote to London's Lord Mayor and six others including Killigrew, asking them to begin the process of raising loans from resident foreigners who had grown fat by dominating trade and paying no tax. The enquiry should quietly inform itself of the wealth and state of these strangers, how the money could be gathered, what each should pay. Later we will give you more direction, without seeming to take former notice from you, to call them before you, the Council promised guilefully. Ten percent would be the going rate of interest.

In this year Burghley died. William Cecil and Harry Killigrew had shared experience of politics dating back to the reign of Henry the Eighth, covering more than sixty years. They had been schooled in the same Cambridge tradition and operated around the edges of power during the reign of Edward the Sixth. Both had withdrawn to the margins during the time of Queen Mary. For forty years under Elizabeth they had worked hand in glove on uncountable tasks, married two sisters and shared the same temperament. Cecil had remained the landlocked operator in the curtained room, Henry the soldier, traveller and castle-handler, shining in the privilege of William's power like an orbiting moon. Now only Killigrew of the old school remained, but his light had not yet been eclipsed.

Two more of Killigrew's sons, Henry and Robert (Robin in Henry's will) and fifth daughter Jaél, were born around the mid nineties. Two daughters of his first marriage were now young wives of Cornish neighbours, Elizabeth married Jonathan Trelawny and Mary married Reginald Mohun, although Mary did not live long. Dorothy, the youngest of Catherine's children, wanted perhaps to gaze into the future as well as into the eyes of a beloved when around 1599 she consulted Simon Forman, the well known astrologer and empiric who performed such a useful role in helping A L Rowse to identify Shakespeare's dark lady.

In 1599, at about the time when the Globe theatre was ready for *King Henry the Fifth,* Henry Killigrew finally gave up his lucrative post of Teller of the Exchequer, having contributed to ensuring that its standards were remarkably good. For a while he had shared the post with Henry Neville, who confirmed that 'by agreement between us I was not to meddle in it, nor to take any benefit of it during his time'. Killigrew had perhaps ceased to be a Gentleman of the Privy Chamber, although William remained in the less senior post of Groom for many years. Henry no doubt judged it wise to remain domiciled close to the centre of national affairs; a Cornish lease of 1599 referred to him as Sir Henry Killigrew of London.

Over the next few years, Harry seems to have encouraged his ward Jonathan Trelawny, twenty-one in 1597, to follow his own example in keeping in with both the two main power-blocks at Court. Jonathan seems to have responded to requests from both Essex and Robert Cecil to use his influence to provide sympathetic members of parliament from Cornwall.

Essex supporter Henry Neville, now knighted and like Jonathan married to one of Killigrew's daughters, became MP for Liskeard in 1597 and two years later was appointed Ambassador to Paris. Jonathan, who was one of the prestigious county MPs in 1597, joined him in the embassy for six months: families passing skills around, dynasties within walls. Elizabeth Trelawny took over the family affairs with her father's aplomb, writing to her cousin Robert Cecil to obtain postponement on sale of the manor of Trelawne until Jonathan could return to buy it.

In 1601 Trelawny offered the Liskeard seat for Cecil to use. This tack may reflect troubles in the Killigrew network. All had seemed well for a new generation poised in their web of mutual interest: the failure of Arwennack need not trouble them. Then, in the autumn and winter of 1600-1, Neville became drastically enmeshed in the final misjudgments of the Paranoid Earl. Foolish, arrogant, increasingly crazed Essex leant right off balance to challenge the Queen's authority in a fashion no-one had dared during forty previous years of her reign. The conspiracy and revolt bubbled up and failed leaving Essex to die for his trouble. Robert Cecil was now more or less supreme under the Crown.

After the collapse of the half-baked insurrection the government ordered Neville to be confined to Sir Henry Killigrew's London house while his possessions were examined. Killigrew was furious with Neville and his anger encompassed Anne also: she was refused admission to the house. Was so much of the web now going to hang ragged, not the edge occupied by salt-caked Fal incompetents but the very centre, occupied by a young man on the threshold of national power? The Lords of the Council, no less, were obliged to temper Harry's fury towards Anne, writing to instruct him 'to receive her in his house and to use her with that countenance and comfort that heretofore he had done'.

This outburst of a father may seem unprincipled, but Henry had witnessed sixty years of Tudor fear, rage and retribution in response to treason.

Although only marginally involved in the conspiracy, Neville was caught up in the Queen's not unreasonable fury. Stripped of all offices he was moved to the Tower. Anne wrote frantic letters to Robert Cecil who was unable to modify the Queen's anger. William Killigrew wrote to Robert Cecil too, commiserating with 'my poor old brother'.

Although Essex was dead, people like Southampton and Neville might have to be reprieved to protect the honour of their class. How could such a shoddy rebellion have occurred? How could so many of the highly placed have gone astray? If such as Neville were allowed to accept the guilt, the very integrity of the Court to which they belonged would be implicated. Scapegoats had to be found, low-life Evil Councillors swimming in an undercurrent of slime, leading others through gutters.

Servants took the rap. Cuffe, a secretary of Essex, 'cunning coiner of all plots', had been accused at the trial of Essex of having entrapped Sir Henry Neville, a 'worthy gentleman', into countenancing the treason. He was 'the sacrificial lamb offered upon the altar of Tudor snobbery, social prejudice and paranoia... evil was by definition low-born' (Smith).

However, nothing could wipe away the fact that the Virgin Queen had been invaded by Essex in her closest privacy, her dignity fatally undermined. The magic which sustained the theatre of monarchy had been decompressed, her mystique would never be fully recreated.

Neville's life was spared but he was fined the massive sum of £5,000 and his career was ruined for the rest of the reign.

Henry Killigrew was not held responsible for his son-in-law. Only a few months later in the spring of 1601 the Queen, still darkened in the shadow of the rebellion, was graciously pleased to sign Jaél's application for English citizenship. This was clearly not an everyday occurrence. The Clerk of the Signet wrote to Jaél 'I have presented to her Majesty the letter to make you an English lady, and she has signed it quickly and with many gracious words'. The Clerk suggested that Henry should make the journey to Court himself to thank the Queen. Jaél wrote back from Lothbury: 'I should not have delayed my reply, but I was waiting for a messenger who, sharing the favour, would have supplied my defects in acknowledging it, but he is too ill to follow your counsel'.

Even in her shock and grief as she watched her dynasty fade towards a whimper, surely the Queen felt some real affection for the dull little man who had first visited her father's Palace in 1545 and known her when she was a child, had been apprenticed in the household which produced perhaps the only man she ever really loved, and had worked in her own cause for over forty years?

After Essex, young energies darted hither and thither seeking live wires. Only the dour unlovely Robert Cecil offered to conduct them towards the Scottish king who was on line to install his camp-followers in the English Court.

Did Henry visit Cornwall in his old age, maybe to enjoy a long stay with the Trelawnys? His will, drafted in 1602, has a strong Cornish emphasis, but he still had no obvious place of residence. It was upheld in later centuries that he had built the fine house which stands on the Ince promontory near Lanrake, but this building, with its four shapely towers, was constructed forty years later by his son Henry, and completed just before the Civil War. Generations later, Celtic rumours accredited old Sir Harry with the competency of incarcerating a woman in each tower.

That greater fire was soon to burn out. Towards the end of February 1603 the Queen was in residence at Richmond, distraught at the death of Lady Nottingham, her close companion, and she excused herself from engagements. At this death 'she has wept extremely and shown an uncommon concern'. She never emerged again from her chamber, sitting silently and refusing to go to bed, becoming increasingly ill and withdrawn.

On 24th March she died, but Harry did not hear that news. On 2nd March, as the Queen sat unmoving at Court, he too had died.

Sir Henry was buried in his local church of St Margaret's, Lothbury, adjacent to his brother's garden and summer house, close by the house William had given to the parson. In April 1604 the fussy, intrusive, careless Vestry Minute Book of that puritan church records that it was 'left to the parson to certify Lady Killigrew that the parish left it to her discretion for the Erectinge of a tombe according to his (Killigrew's) desire and if it pleased her to bestow anything upon the poor, att her pleasure, and no somme should be demanded of her'. A later entry confirms 'For Sir Henry Killigrew's tombe it was seen by the parish and agreed that 2 should go to the Lady to see what she would give but none were named'.

In the seven lengthy pages of his will - which can still be viewed at the Public Record Office in London - Harry had taken great pains to protect the income of his wife and to safeguard his young sons. The estates of Lanrake and Bottlet were to provide the bulk of the necessary income: there is no mention of Hendon or Lothbury properties. As eldest Joseph, just ten years old when Henry died, should be the proud recipient of his 'best sets of hangings'.

Killigrew endowed five Cornish parishes, including Budock, where the elegant memorial to brother Sir John and Lady Mary Of The Chairs survives to this day. He left money to Kathleen his chambermaid for her 'long pains and rare in attending my children', also to his servant John 'in recompense of his pains with me in my late sickness'. He remembers the French Huguenot church in London, and his will also reminds his French mother-in-law that she had never paid him 2,000 crowns promised at his marriage.

The trustees of the will are his brother William, brother in law Francis Godolphin, and neighbours William Treffry of Fowey and young Richard Carew of Antony - a Cornish vigil at the last.

In the year of Killigrew's death Shakespeare became a Groom of the Chamber alongside William Killigrew, and the stage at the Globe rang to the first performance of Alls Well That Ends Well - ironic title for a disenchanted comment on the thwarting of personal fulfilment by the times' unjust intrusions.

Those who mourned Henry may have felt that by and large the times had treated him well. In the public domain he had witnessed the acceptance of many religious ideals which he had cherished fifty years earlier, although the pace of change had now stopped. He had contributed to the considerable strengthening of England within Europe. Although the country's internal administration and taxation was still largely unredeemed, especially locally, the running of the Exchequer was in considerable good order.

The personal dimension of his life was also successful. He had never risen to one of the highest offices, but this is unlikely to have troubled him. He had side-stepped disaster and made positive gains. In a dangerous era he had avoided the unpopularity which followed Dudley to his grave, loss of judgment which terminated Essex, Hatton's frustrations, overwork and poverty which befell Walsingham, the disgrace which unseated Ralegh and Davison. He had never passed an involuntary spell inside the Tower.

The new branch of the family which he had established was nationally respected if not markedly wealthy. His heirs did not however emulate his high achievements. Young Sir Joseph had few years to enjoy his father's best hangings, dying in his early twenties; second son Henry fought gallantly for the King in the Civil War and died of wounds sustained at the siege of Pendennis; Robin outlived them both.

Jonathan Trelawny also died young and disastrously, only a year after old Sir Harry, as a result of a fit of coughing during a sitting of Parliament. But Jaél lived on until the 1630s and remarried, and Sir William Killigrew stayed influential at Court until his death in 1622 - he must have been around ninety. Neville also regained his position in the new reign, so Anne did not suffer permanent disgrace.

In the immediate aftermath of his death, few found time to study the achievements of Harry Killigrew and his generation. Holding Robert Cecil's map, King James Stuart set off on the road southwards and prepared to clamp his no less idiosyncratic dynasty onto the young century.

REFERENCES AND FURTHER READING

In addition to general histories of aspects of the Tudor period, the following have been helpful, most especially Professor Miller's book on Killigrew which contains a full bibliography.

1. **Manuscript.**

    Killigrew's will, PRO. PCC 26 Bolein

2. **Printed sources.**

    Official records for the period:

    > Acts of the Privy Council,
    >
    > Calendars of State Papers Domestic and Foreign,
    >
    > Calendars of Hatfield Mss

3. **Secondary works.**

Beckinsale, P.W.	Burghley, Tudor Statesman. Macmillan 1967
Bindoff, S.	Tudor England. Pelican 1950.
Byrne, M St Claire, ed.	The Lisle Letters, Vols I - VI. University of Chicago Press, 1981. Abridged, Secker and Warburg 1983, Penguin 1985.
Carew, R.	See Halliday, Rowse 1987.
Carnsew, W.	See Rowse 1987.
Collinson, P.	The Elizabethan Puritan Movement. Cape 1967.
du Maurier, D.	Golden Lads: A Study of Anthony Bacon, Francis and their Friends. Gollanz, 1975.
Halliday, F.E, ed.	Richard Carew of Antony: The Survey of Cornwall, etc. Melrose 1953.
Hasler, P W.	The House of Commons, 1558 - 1603. HMSO 1981.
Haynes, A.	Invisible Power: The Elizabethan Secret Services, 1570 - 1603. Sutton 1992.

Loades, D.M.	Two Tudor Conspiracies. Cambridge UP, 1965.
MacCaffrey, W.T.	The Shaping of the Elizabethan Regime. Cape 1969.
Miller, Amos.	Sir Henry Killigrew: Elizabethan Soldier and Diplomat. Leicester University Press, 1963.
Rowse, A.L.	Tudor Cornwall. Revised edition, Cape 1968.
Rowse, A.L. (1).	Richard Carew, Antiquary;
(2).	The Diary of William Carnsew, Country Gentleman;
	In Court and Country, Studies in Tudor Social History. Harvester, 1987.
Smith, Lacey Baldwin.	Treason in Tudor England: Politics and Paranoia. Cape 1986.
Wilson, D.	Sweet Robin: A Biography of Robert Dudley, Earl of Leicester. Hamish Hamilton 1981.

INDEX

INDEX